THE HEART OF THE SOMERSET LEVELS

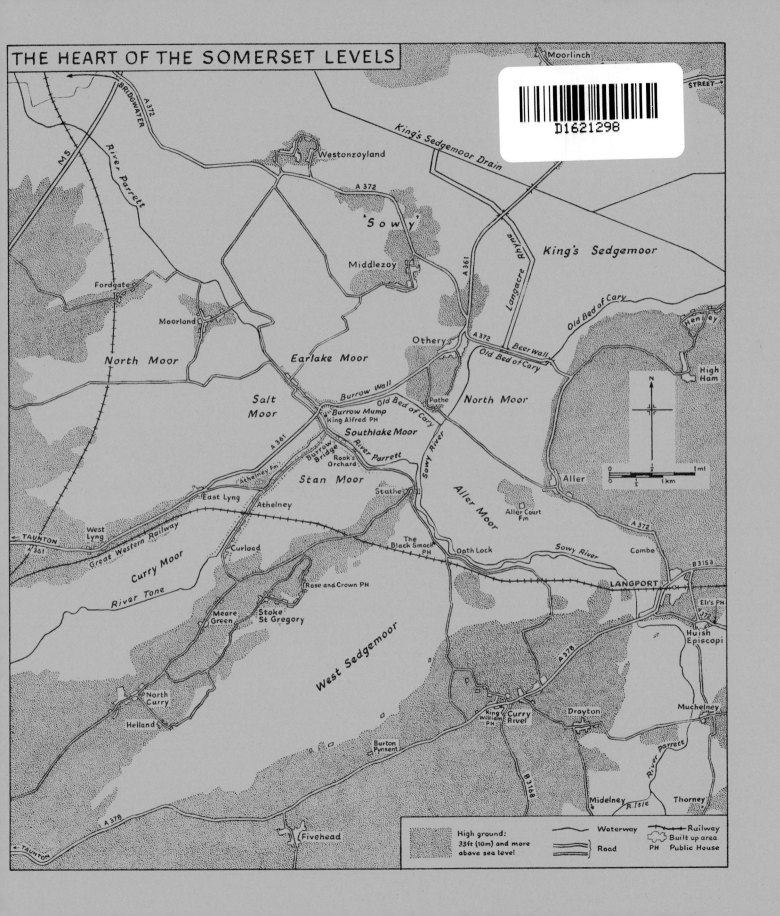

Moorlinch

STREET →

BRIDGWATER

A 372

M 5

River Parrett

King's Sedgemoor Drain

Westonzoyland

A 372

'Sowy'

King's Sedgemoor

Middlezoy

A 361

Langacre Rhyne

Fordgate

Moorland

North Moor

Earlake Moor

Othery

A 372

Beer Wall

Old Bed of Cary

Henley

Old Bed of Cary

High Ham

Salt Moor

Burrow Wall

A 361

Old Bed of Cary

Pathe

North Moor

N

Burrow Mump
King Alfred PH

Southlake Moor

River Parrett

Sowy River

Athelney Fm.

Burrow Bridge

Rook's Orchard

Stan Moor

Stathe

Aller Moor

Aller

0   ½   1 ml
0   ½   1 km

East Lyng

Athelney

Aller Court Fm

A 372

West Lyng

Great Western Railway

Curload

The Black Smock PH

Oath Lock

Sowy River

Combe

← TAUNTON

A 361

Curry Moor

River Tone

Rose and Crown PH

LANGPORT

B 3153

Elr's PH

Meare Green

Stoke St Gregory

Huish Episcopi

West Sedgemoor

North Curry

A 378

Drayton

Muchelney

Helland

King William PH

Curry Rivel

Burton Pynsent

B 3168

River Parrett

Midelney

R. Isle

Thorney

A 378

← TAUNTON

Fivehead

High ground:
33ft (10m) and more
above sea level

Waterway

Road

Railway

Built up area

PH   Public House

WETLAND
Life in the Somerset Levels

WETLAND
Life in the Somerset Levels

Patrick Sutherland and Adam Nicolson

MICHAEL JOSEPH
LONDON

First published in Great Britain by
Michael Joseph Limited
44 Bedford Square, London WC1
1986

British Library Cataloguing in Publication Data

Nicolson, Adam
   Wetland: Life in the Somerset Levels.
   1. Somerset Levels (England)—Description
   and travel
   I. Title   II. Sutherland, Patrick
   914.23'8   DA670.S4/

   ISBN 0–7181–2603–3

Filmset by Wilmaset, Birkenhead, Wirral
Printed and bound in Great Britain by
Butler and Tanner, Frome, Somerset

Our thanks are due to:

Ivan Arnold at Fisons; Norman Baker; George Bawden; Ray Beck; Helen and Graham Beere; Lewis Boobyer; Walter Boucher; Alf Brewer; Maisie and Walter Brown; Martyn Brown; Michael and Utta Brown; John Browning; Phyllis Champion; Anne, Chris, Jonathan and Philip Coate; Don Coate; Emrys Coate; Netty Coate; Ruth Colbeck; Professor J. M. Coles; Rob Coles; George Cotty; Fred Cousins; Clifford Crossman; Stan Dare; Ginger David; Stan Derham; David Drew; Mark Durston; Stan Durston; Liz and Geoff Evans; Clifford Fear; Pip Gibbons; John Gould; Mr F. Griffiths; Stan Hall; Dr Hancock at the STNC; Jimmy Hartland; Mike Hayes; John Hector; Nigel Hector; Ena Hembrow; Francis Hembrow; Jim and Philip Heyward; Aubrey Hill; Tom Hodge; Julian Honeybun; Stan Honeybun; David House; Dick House; Mr and Mrs Norman House; John Humphreys; David Illingworth; Morris Ingram; Dr Brian Johnston at the NCC; Charles Keirle; Max King; Philippa Legge; Bob Lock; Fred Lock; Les Lock; Sandra Lovelace; Sharon Loxton; Tony Mailey; Alfred Male; Ken Male; Leonard Meade; Julie Miller; Geoff Moxey; Malcolm Musgrave; Wallace Musgrave; Joan Norris; David Perrin; Kenny and Sylvia Pimms; Tim Pollard at the Community Council for Somerset; Dr Michael Richards; George Rivet; Brendan Sellick; Sue and Chris Southwell; Keith Speller; Arthur 'Sam' Stuckey; Mabel Stuckey; Mr L. H. Sweet; Ray Sweet; Julian Temperley; Bob Thorne; Joan and Florence Tucker; John Uppham; John Vowles; Matt Walker at the Newbridge Plant Company; Angela Wickenden; Roger Wilkins; Rob Williams; Harold, Dennis and Richard Wright; to Jenny Dereham at Michael Joseph for all her enthusiasm and support; and to Charlie Langford, Harold Meade and Charlie Showers, all of whom have now died.

This book is dedicated to Harold Hembrow.

When the water in the River Parrett stays high for a few hours, penned up there by the spring tides in the Bristol Channel, or full of the floodwaters from rain in Dorset, it seeps out through the river bank and into Harold Hembrow's garden in Burrow Bridge. The water soaks up into the vegetables, floating their leaves, and washes at the roots of the old roses. No water comes into the house itself, which is only a yard or two from the river bank, but the line of damp on the wallpaper climbs towards the ceiling throughout the spring and early summer each year, in a ragged brown graph of the season, lifting above the furniture at Easter, reaching the top of the windows by June. As he says:

'It's only the heat. The heat's to push it up. And then perhaps it'll keep up there for a week till it all dries. And then in the winter it'll come back again. I don't take no notice of it. It's no good to. A lot of the houses along here have all been altered since. The next one along they paid £350, was it, to stop the damp. I told him straight. He said, bugger, he couldn't make it out, this was about the first one he ever had, to my knowledge, that wouldn't come dry. Whatever you do, you will not stop it, I said. I don't care how many holes you drill, you will not stop it. So he drilled another lot of holes to inject another lot of stuff in. It won't *ever* work. What was it under water for? Six months, wasn't it, in '29/30? Everything, it soaked right through everything in that time, right through. It's never going to dry out. No matter whatever you do.

'All houses, I reckon, next to this river, *should* be damp. It is the way. A lot of them say we've had this done, we've had that and still every so often we get the damp to come back. And, yes, it always will come back. Unless you knock them right away round, put in a couple of layers of asphalt, but in time that'll go. That'll rot away in time. And then you'll be back to square one. When Kathleen was alive, every two years it was wallpapered. Now the wallpaper's coming off with the damp. She was exactly like me. She didn't care who it was; if she had something to say, she was going to say it. That's the way. She always wanted new paper every two years, but I haven't changed it since she died and now it's coming off.'

Wetness is not a substance but a quality that seeps and leaks into everything like a stain. Wetness blurs and softens any margins, making distinctions indistinct. When Richard Jefferies lay on Liddington Hill in Wiltshire, with the solid chalk under his back and even the water in the dewponds made thicker by the rock that had dissolved in them, he felt himself pushed up and out of the earth by the chalk, made prominent by its solidity. But the low wet moors of the Somerset Levels, thick with their waters, are the negative, the feminine of that. They are the most female of landscapes and if you lie and sleep there on a summer afternoon, you will dream not of prominence but of absorption, of the half-liquid jelly beneath you, shifting in all its ambiguities, curling its flesh around you in the soft kiss of an insect-eating fungus.

If a tractor drives past, the loose suspension of the peat will shiver and ripple its bellies under you, wobbling the earth in a slow-motion swell. In the days before tractors, horses that went out on the moor needed sacks around their hooves if they were not to sink into the fields. Others, too sharp-footed – the best Levels horses had feet like frying pans – would quite slowly subside where they stood, their four legs slipping into the peat like the pins of a plug into a socket. And there they would be stuck in their sloppy, hopeless prison. It still happens with the cows that have fallen in the ditches. Tractors have to pull them out with a rope around their horns. At first, there is no give. The cow remains stranded in the peat as a giant, legless, beached, black and white seal. The wet creates a suction around the body, holding it in there, while the poor animal's stuck-out jaw and neck take all the strain. The tractor judders. Its wheels cut into the turf and the cow preserves an appalled silence until, in

Harold Hembrow at home in Rook's Orchard, Burrow Bridge.
'You'll never get rid of the damp. The damp's in the place.'

The Levels live up to their name; no landscape is more conducive to sleep.

The last of a flood on Tadham Moor; a gradual, interrupted and unfinished sorting of land from water.

Frogbit and duckweed disrupt the reflections of the bullock faces in a rhyne on Aller Moor, where for over six centuries the keeping of cattle and the control of water has shaped the wetland.

one instant delivering *collop*, she is up and out and stinking, standing in the field, coated in the deep sulphurous peat of the moor. Wetness, not a substance but a quality, the condition of life.

It happens to the houses too. Modern planning regulations demand that any new building on the Levels should be founded on concrete piles, sunk forty feet or more through the soft ground to the hidden rock. What you see is no more than the top half of a building on stilts. This is good for local builders; it is said to double the cost of a house. Victorian farmers used to press whole shiploads of fir trees into the ground before building, dropping them in there, yards at a time, with a horse-driven pile-driver, but poorer houses had no such foundation. You see them all over the Levels, part-lurched into the ooze, the ghosts of old doorways that have tipped on the diagonal, rubbed out and replaced with a modern vertical. Into these houses, as you step inside, you step a foot or two down.

Of all the demonstrations of life on the wet, the most spectacular is Bow Street in Langport, the main street of the market town at the south-eastern corner of the Levels. The houses are built along either side of a twelfth-century causeway across the valley of the Parrett, which narrows here to no more than a passage between the hills. The street is built with all the solidity of provincial significance, with copybook Tuscan and awkward caryatids in the blue lias, with banks lined up next to libraries and offices, but as you look down the street you will notice that each side leans back away from it, out of true, settling down into the soft ground of the moor and widening their eaves to the sky.

The excavation of an empty lot on Bow Street in the summer of 1985 revealed a series of triangular sections fanned upwards since the thirteenth century, in which each new floor, thick with fishbones, charcoal and oysters, had slipped back into the inexorable wet and then, on rebuilding, had been made up with rubble to restore the horizontal.

Wetness is not a substance but a quality, the condition of life. 'You'll never get rid of the damp,' Harold Hembrow said. 'The damp's *in* the place.'

Now you must imagine yourself suspended a mile above this sponge landscape – in a balloon, perhaps – and that you have been hanging there for ten thousand years while the centuries have flicked past and the modern physique of the Somerset Levels has appeared beneath you. It will be a history of emergence, of a gradual, interrupted and unfinished sorting of land from water, part natural, part human.

In the beginning, there is the rim of hills. The Mendips, the north Dorset downlands, the Black Downs, the Brendons and the Quantocks – a rough horseshoe – enclose a basin in which rivers have cut valleys and left the harder rocks standing out as ridges and knolls. The land stretches out beyond them in a swampy waste as far as the hills in Wales. The Somerset rivers are tributaries of the Severn and all of them wander indolently across the plain, leaking out into boggy pools and shifting in the confusion of no gradient. After about ten thousand years, the weather improves and the sea rises, pushing into the swamplands, filling the valleys for about three thousand years. A steady dull rain of muds and silts brought down by the rivers falls on the valley floors and blankets them in clay.

The sea-water begins to retreat in about 4,500 B.C. A broad, low ridge of clay builds up along the shore of what is now the Bristol Channel and a yellow bolster of sand dunes thickens on the seaward side of the ridge. The clay is no more than a few feet high and a mile or two wide but it completes the enclosure of the inland moors, preventing easy drainage from the hills to the sea. The rivers flowing down through the Levels – the Axe, the Brue, the Cary, the Parrett and the Tone, find that their way out to sea is virtually blocked and often flood over the corrugated, clay-lined saucer. The first reed swamps spring up in the pools left by the flooding. The Levels are no more than part-land, a land between two waters: between the surge of sea-floods in from the Bristol Channel and the choking of land-floods from rain on the surrounding hills.

Islands of rock and sand and the long solid finger of the Polden Hills, which divides the Levels in two, rise above

Southlake Moor below Burrow Mump and, in the distance, the Polden Hills. This is the physique of the Levels: low, flat, wet moors surrounded by ridges and interrupted by hills — the islands in a dried-up, prehistoric marsh.

A light winter flood on Aller Moor: part-land, poised between tides
from the Bristol Channel and the river-floods from rain on the
surrounding hills.

Clifford Fear drags weed from a flooded ditch on Tealham Moor: a landscape of control and vigilance.

the wetland. This distinction between the ridges and islands of high ground and the flat moorland between them – the webbing between the bones of a duck's foot – is the deciding shape of the Somerset Levels. Parish boundaries nearly always run across the division, taking in both sorts of land, low and wet as well as high and dry, the double resource of a marshland/dryland economy. The world changes as you lift even two or three feet above the moor, from floodable to flood-free. It is the difference between the molten and the mould and, if you had to find one word to describe the Levels, you could say it was a *poured* landscape. The corrugations of the hill-ridges are all that hold it in place. There is one (or two: the Rose and Crown in Stoke St Gregory has copied it) great demonstration of this essential structure of the Levels. In the King William at Curry Rivel, only a few feet away from the public bar and still inside the room, there is a glassed-over well. Stools are arranged around it and the glass does as a table-top. Beneath half-empty pints of cider and an ashtray is the lit-up shaft of the well. It is dry-walled for a few feet and then cut through the natural rock to the small pool of water, which for some reason is always shimmering, many yards below. It is the memory of water that is visible through the pub floor, the distance from water which has put the village and the pub up here on the hill in the first place, separated from that water by the foundation of the rock in the shaft itself.

From your balloon view, the first evidence of human beings now appears on the high ground. Hazel and ashwoods are coppiced. There is a clearance of elm and alder. The first wooden trackways are laid out across the swamp, but these are no more than tiny filaments in the grand natural development of the place. For about a thousand years, the reeds grow, die and fall into the water. In the absence of oxygen and bacteria, they are preserved there to become the first layers of peat thickening above the clay.

By about 3,500 B.C. – but this is a patchy, interrupted process, occurring at different times in different places – the dead plants have grown thick enough for the ground surface to have emerged above the water and, on these damp islands, a sudden rash of fenwood erupts, at first with the pioneers – birch, willow and alder – and in some places becoming firm and dry enough to take ash, oak and elm.

This phase, particularly in the Levels north of the Poldens where drainage is most difficult, lasts no more than a few centuries. Heavy rain around 3,000 B.C. begins to create the very wet conditions for a raised bog. Sphagnum moss, heather and cotton-grass now coat the great warts of the bog in a tweedy stipple, interrupted by an occasional myrtle bush and a stagnant, acid pool.

Now and then for a moment the sea floods over and islands the knolls, dropping tons of mud on to the edges of the bog and sweeping away the earlier vegetation. From your balloon, there is a constant flickering on the surface, like the shimmering in turned silk, as new ponds appear, as old ponds thicken and fill, as drier patches acquire their trees, grow damp again and are swept away in a flood. The two elements, the land and water, shift and exchange, muddle in with each other and then separate, as the creeping growth – of floating aquatics, the sudden flash of duckweed on a pond, of lilies rooted in the stream bed climbing to the surface, of the endless variety of sedges and rushes and reeds pushing the banks in towards the centre – tries to re-establish the solid in this would-be liquid world, before the floods come again and sweep wide tracts of the place away.

In amongst this breathing of the wilderness, with its own diseases and flourishings and forms of decay, the work of men appears as no more than another slight fluttering in the landscape. A constant succession of trackways is laid across the marsh as the peat accumulates – and each one is engulfed in turn. Not until the Iron Age, in about 400 B.C., do people come down from the ridges and islands to live on the edges of the bog itself. Lake villages are established near Glastonbury and Meare.

The villages are abandoned before the coming of the Romans, as conditions grow worse again. A Roman road is driven along the crest of the Poldens towards the port on the estuary of the Parrett at Combwich. It is possible that

A flooded fenwood near Godney, where birch, willow and alder have
colonised the surface of the peat.

the first bright line of a drainage ditch on the very eastern edges of the marsh near the buildings of a Roman villa now appears beneath you. The evidence for it is uncertain and there is no doubt that the great expanse of the marsh, 250 square miles, remains unclaimed. The last great irruption from the sea occurs in about A.D. 250 and the raised bog stops growing, for reasons unknown, about a hundred and fifty years later. It is at this phase, with the steady rhythm beneath you of winter flooding and summer drying, a regular, metronomic beating of the marshland pulse, each year re-enacting the history of emergence, that the Levels first enter written history.

On one of the smallest sandy islands called Athelney, no more than 35 feet above the surrounding flatness, King Alfred hid from the Danes. It is the great symbolic moment in the history of the Levels. The defeated king travelled 'in difficulties through the woods and fen fastnesses' to the last safe fragment of his kingdom, 'surrounded on all sides by very great swampy and impassable marshes, so that no one can approach it by any means except in punts'. Asser's description makes it a landscape of despair and isolation, a low point from which Alfred's later, victorious, law-giving life could expand. From the tiny, hedged-about and crisis-ridden island of Athelney, Alfred moves on to victory over the Danes, to a dictated peace at Wedmore further north in the Levels, and an enforced baptism of the Danish king at Aller, just across the Parrett from Athelney. The shape of the Levels provides the perfect set for this drama of resistance and resurgence. Nothing could articulate the story better than an archipelago in the marsh and nothing suits the landscape of the Levels more than the story of a beleaguered king finally triumphing over a foreign enemy.

These are invisible scurryings from the balloon. At Athelney itself, there is now a farm and a nineteenth-century monument to the king. Nothing survives of the monastery founded by Alfred in thanks for his deliverance. But if Alfred was grateful, the other Saxons were not and – this reveals the slum-status of the Levels at the time – none could be persuaded to live on the bog-surrounded island as monks. Years before, as the Saxons had advanced down the Fosse Way, the British had retreated to the marshes for safety and the Saxons had failed to pursue them there. Now again the only monks who could be found to staff the monastery were foreigners. Asser himself, a Welshman from Pembrokeshire, felt nothing but contempt for those flesh-loving Saxons who refused to leave the richer, dryer lands 'up off', as they now say, blaming their depravity on 'too great an abundance of riches of every kind'.

Despite the monastery at Athelney and the far larger abbey at Glastonbury, the landscape itself remained virtually unchanged. Place-names preserve that earlier geography. Over the maps of the Levels, the names of villages which once occupied islands in the marsh have kept in their suffix -y or -ey, the remains of the old English ēg or iēg, meaning island. They are like a string of adjectives describing the place: Thorney, Horsey, Midelney, Muchelney (the large island), Bradney (the broad). Athelney means the island of the princes and many others preserve the names of individual Saxons – Godney, Marchey, Pitney. The large sandy island separating the Parrett basin from King's Sedgemoor used to be called Sowy, elided in Somerset English to Zoy. Three villages now occupy the island, Westonzoyland, Middlezoy and Othery – the western, middle and simply the other village on Sowy. The name of another separate and smaller island to the north-west is now written on maps as Chedzoy, meaning Cedd's island. The earliest form of this name is Ched*sie*, and only later, under the influence of the nearby Sowy-Zoy, was that last syllable changed. This would be of no more than academic interest if it were not for an extraordinary piece of continuity which has bypassed all the official cartographers and namers of places. The 'oy' in Westonzoyland and Middlezoy is pronounced as it is written but Chedzoy is universally called Ched*sey*.

The spirit of a place will always last longest in the names of its rivers and their names are nearly always older than those of the towns and villages on their banks. The name of the Parrett is too ancient; it cannot be explained. The Cary has the same root as the River Cher

The Parrett on the left meets the Tone on the right near Burrow Bridge: two of the slimiest rivers in Europe which regularly slop over into their surrounding flood plains. Ironically, the safest place on which to build a house is the bank itself, above all but the highest floods.

in France – something to be loved, a Celtic affection. The meanings of Brue and Tone are pre-Saxon too but are the most inappropriate river-names in the country. Brue, a sluggish stewed swamp of a river, probably means 'brisk' or 'vigorous'. The Tone, a flat tidal ditch with slimy grey banks, is a derivative of a word meaning 'roaring'. Only in the worst of floodtimes, as people discovered in 1929 and 1960, can the Tone justify its etymology. Only the Axe has a name that is appropriate. Like Usk and Esk with which it is cognate, Axe means 'water'.

By the thirteenth century, five and a half thousand years have passed in which men have adapted themselves to the natural rhythm of water in these marshlands. The dryland has provided them with crops and a sure-footing, the wet with game, firewood, fish and – in summer – lush grazing. The name of Somerset itself is the Anglo Saxon for these summer pastures, the Somer Saete. But as the thirteenth century slides up under your balloon, with only six centuries left out of the sixty in which men have been farming on the Levels, a sudden change occurs. Suddenly on the dull land, there is the sparkle of straight ditches, at first only at the edges of the islands, but then spreading – not gradually but in bursts – a whole moor there, another here, like the lights coming on in different rooms of a building. Rivers are straightened and redirected. Weirs, watergates and sluices are built. In three great phases, in the thirteenth century, between 1770 and 1830 and since the beginning of the Second World War – with long periods of hopelessness and negligence in between – the landscape of the Somerset Levels is transformed. From an unmade, it is turned into a made place. Those straight lines are the

map of interference, of shaping, of putting to deliberate use. It is no longer a question of gathering what the place can offer but of bending it to a will and a need.

A new and fragile geography was created. From being the most dictated-to and determinist of landscapes, the Levels became the most vulnerable and maintained. Nowhere except an irrigated patch of desert or a small clearing in an equatorial rain forest will return to its natural state more quickly than a drained swamp. It is the country where vigilance is king. A drainage ditch, if neglected, will be solid with plants in five or six years. A sea-wall left untended will allow the next surge to break in fourteen miles or more, with all its sterilising load of salt. Even modern underdrains can be clogged with peat in fifteen years. A river bank will wash away in flood.

If you walk through the meadows here in early summer, along the banks of the Parrett, say, or the Brue, nothing is more insistent than the surge of vegetable life around you and nothing more obvious than the need of men to trim it back. Summer is a visible thickening of the place, fed by its own wet, in the plump leaves of the comfrey bunches on the river bank, in the extraordinary resurgence of life after a ditch has been cleared to the naked mud, in the three or even four cuts of silage a year which the more modern farmers can take off these fields. The tall willow wands that are planted in wide beds on the moors are the most extraordinary demonstrations of the life in the place. They are cut to the ground each winter but by the autumn they have grown eight feet high. A withy can grow three inches on a good hot day and – magically – continue at night, so that the rustle you hear on a warm still evening in July is not the slightest of breezes picked

Kingcup fringes a rhyne on Tealham Moor. These ditches are both the veins and the arteries of the Levels, irrigating the fields in summer and in winter carrying away the excess water.

Ken Male and Les Lock, working for the Wessex Water Authority, gather the cut rushes on the River Isle: shearing the great summer growth on the Levels.

Estuarine mud near the mouth of the Parrett. Here are the Levels in the making, as they would have looked when the sea first withdrew from them about 6,500 years ago.

up by the leaves of the withies and unnoticed on the skin, but the rustle of growth itself.

The Levels sprout their fantastic summer beard. Summer adds another dimension to the winter flatness and people then shear it off, control, contain and use it. That is the character of the Levels: the thickness and constancy with which the nature of the place comes up – there is a buoyancy, nothing mean in it – and the discipline and rigidity with which men, if they are to live there at all, must hold that wildness down.

If you look closely you will notice that it is a locked landscape. There are locks everywhere, even miles from roads or houses. Locks on chains around the control wheel of a sluice; locks on the doors to the control boxes of tilting dams; locks to the pumping stations; locks on the chests where the winch handles are stored; locks on the machinery of the great clyses that shut out the high tide at the mouths of the rivers, changing the world at that point from the eel skin of the estuarine mud into the sorted, controlled landscape of meadow and water. The chains and the locks and the constant cutting back and shearing in the summer are both witness to the paradox of the Levels: it is a landscape where the destructive power of nature – in the form of rampant water and overpowering vegetation – is extraordinarily near at hand; and at the same time, a place where the human moulding and manipulation of the landscape is most obvious, far plainer here than on Great Gable or in the park at Petworth.

This place that drools water, that depends on water, where water must be contained and controlled, has its own definite physics in which water is both malleable and pervasive. First, there is the inadequacy of the rivers. Between Langport and Bridgwater, a distance of eleven and a half miles, the bed of the River Parrett drops 11 feet 6 inches, a gradient of 1 in 5280. This is the most grudging of invitations to a river from the sea. The Brue does even worse – about 1 in 7900 – and the King's Sedgemoor Drain, the new course for the River Cary dug in 1794, worst of all at about 1 in 10,500, or a drop of little more than six inches a mile. In places, the beds of these hopeless rivers are actually level with the surrounding moors, so that there can be no drainage by gravitation from the moor into the river. If not for the raised banks on either side, the rivers would simply not exist. As it is, the repeated over-flowing of silt-laden waters in the past has created natural levées – now reinforced – which are good enough for an average flow but inadequate when conditions move even slightly beyond the normal.

But no winter passes without the normal becoming utterly irrelevant. The Levels – and this bears repeating – are between two waters – the rain on the hills which cup them and the tides in the sea which borders them. When high water from both sides meet, the land floods. More than 800 square miles of upland drain into the 250 square miles of the Levels. It so happens that the nine highest recorded rainfalls within twenty-four hours in England between 1865 and 1956 all fell on these hills, suddenly gorging the rivers of the Levels, turning them varicose in a matter of hours. If there were no tides, these rivers might serve their purpose, but the reach of the tide in the Bristol Channel is enormous. The mean highwater springs, about 20 feet above the Ordnance Datum at Newlyn, come level with the coastal clay belt and rise about 10 feet *higher* than the average inland peat moors. A storm surge can add 8 feet to that. In the lowest part of the moors in the Brue basin, a really exceptional tide will be 20 feet or more above the level of the land.

The only means of preventing the sea-water pushing miles inland up the rivers are the great doors called clyses which were fixed across the mouth of the Brue at Highbridge as early as 1485. The King's Sedgemoor Drain was blocked off in 1794, the Axe in 1806 and the Huntspill, a large artificial drain, in 1944. Only the Parrett has no clyse. Its estuary is too wide. The clyse doors are the great Canute gestures of the Levels, the grandest of all the efforts to shut the Levels off from the sea. The Brue clyse at Highbridge is the best. It is a nineteenth-century replacement for its medieval predecessor and is set into a thick white granite dam across the bed of the river. There are two pairs of beamed oak doors, slimed with sea-mud on the seaward side, caught up with river weed and sticks on the other. It is the simplest of technologies: the pressure of the flood tide forces the clyse shut into the mitre of lock gates; and the ebb releases them. They are the clearest Levels image of separation, of sorting land from water.

The clyse will prevent sea-water from pushing up inland but will also stop land-water – as the tide itself would have done – from running out to sea. This tide-lock will last four and a half hours, during which the fresh water will continue to flow. If there is to be no flooding, the river must be able to accommodate 16,200 times its flow per second. When the river is high, there is no chance and the Levels flood.

In the early morning of Saturday, 7 December 1929, at about three o'clock, after heavy continuous rain for weeks and during a strong westerly gale, the River Tone burst its right bank in a cottage garden near Athelney station. The previous Wednesday, at a meeting in the Charter Hall, Bridgwater, Mr Haile, Engineer to the Somerset Drainage Commissioners, had explained, with the help of maps and drawings, '. . . that the Rivers Parrett and Tone, which meet, as you know, at their confluence above Burrow Bridge, are incapable of dealing with the works they are called on to perform during flood periods' Nobody could remember such continuous rain. The Signal Shop in Bridgwater advertised radios in the *Mercury*: 'Beastly Stuff This Water. Thank Goodness My Aerial Is Still Uncovered . . . Wireless Keeps Me In Touch With The World.'

The river banks had been patrolled all week, night and day. The Rev H. Jackson had joined in the vigil. Dangerous spots where the bank was washing were reinforced with sandbags, but the water had stayed high for longer than expected. A mile or two from Athelney, in the lock-keeper's cottage at Oath on the Parrett, Fred Lock was woken by his wife in the blackest part of the night. ' "Hark at that water out there," she says to me. We could feel the vibrations, we could feel it humming up through the house. "That water's going over the top," she says. There was a *rush* on. The whole place was shaking with it. Not the rain we'd had here. No. The rain we'd had miles up. All the water's got to come down through here. She knew it was coming in her sleep. If a stranger was here. living and didn't know the wheresabouts and all that, he wouldn't know where he's to. But we knew every bloody moment of it, didn't we? If you've been here as many years as I have, you don't want to be told, see.'

Early on the Friday evening, the sandbags had run out. The bank in Mrs Miller's garden in Athelney had been repaired years before but the piles had rotted and the gales had blown water on to the landward side of the bank, where the soft garden soil had been washed away. Once the sandbags were exhausted, it was certain that the banks would go. 'Among the roaring of winds and waters,' the *Mercury* man reported, 'disaster, unpreventable and complete, fell upon the little village of Athelney, as the bank gave way, and a broad brown cataract, with a lengthening roar, leapt across the road. Mr Herbert Crossman of Stoke, Mr Jack Hembrow of Stathe, Mr Herbert Hembrow of Burrow Bridge, Mr Richard Dare and Mr Jack Gillard watched as the river cut its way through the embankment, as the Tone surged like a mountain torrent over Mrs Miller's garden shed, ten feet high.'

Every house in Athelney, Stathe and Curload had water in it. Many of the families sheltered in the chapels at Stathe and Stoke St Gregory. Walls of houses collapsed. Others only tilted. People lost hay and potatoes. Trains of cider barrels floated off across the flood. The wads of tied-up withies drifted in rafts around the moorland fields. Furniture washed out of the houses. A chicken house full of dead fowl was discovered wedged up in the branches of a willow. A large black sow was seen swimming across Warmoor with a chicken in its mouth. The Bishop of Bath and Wells made a tour in a boat and then made out a cheque for £50. The *Mercury* said: 'One is confident that the proverbial sportsmanship and Christian charity of the general public in Somerset will extend a helping hand to these unfortunate withy

Harold Hembrow and Fred Lock on the sluice gates at Oath, where in the great flood of 1929 Fred Lock woke up in the night to feel the whole structure quivering and thrumming with the weight of water coming down the Parrett.

growers.' An appeal for rubber boots went out. The Reverend Jackson said he wanted to get all of England interested. In one house in Stathe, the dining-room piano was seen bumping up against the ceiling. In another, a cat and a canary watched each other across a deserted, watery room. Bread was handed up on the points of a hay-fork to families on the upper floors.

Harold Hembrow, who was sixteen at the time, and eleven other members of his family, stayed upstairs at Rook's Orchard in Burrow Bridge while the floodwater swilled about below. 'The flood was lovely. You get on up there and no matter which way you looked it was just like it was years ago. Just water, just like the sea, lovely. Some of the gates you could see in the middle of nowhere, some were right under. It was rough, lovely, like the sea.

'Nobody had no money. There was no work with the flood and it lasted till the spring. Nobody couldn't buy nothing. Nobody had the money to buy it. If you had a shilling in your pocket, you went to the pub. If you didn't you couldn't.

'But, do you know, you could go in a boat from Burrow to Stoke, two miles over dry land? And we fetched a hogshead of cider from Lyng in a boat, fifty-six gallons at sixpence a gallon, and had it upstairs here. Nearly every house had a fireplace upstairs for cooking in the winter floods. Only a little tiny snotty-arsed little grate. You couldn't roast nothing. It all had to be boiled. Boiled meat, fried meat. It was a *glorious* time. We had a hard time, but it was a good time. Like if you go into the King Alfred here: you take the sweet with the bitter.

'But the Hembrows are a wild breed, I suppose. My father was worse than what I was. And the youngest, he's worse than what Father was. There's only one bloody breed of us. You know we're full of electricity? If I take a jersey off at night, it *sparkles* with the electricity. And I've never been able to wear a watch that works because of it. That's because of the breed.

'Well, after the water had been in Stanmoor a week or so, Father decided to do something about it. He had Uncle Sam Winchester up here and said: "Why keep it in here when it would go out the back there, into the Parrett?" The river bank was keeping it in, see? The biggest part of the water in Stanmoor could be let out that way. Now. Years ago you weren't allowed to cut the bank or nothing. You didn't dare look at the bloody thing, let alone touch him. They was frightened to death to bloody touch the thing. So there was a River Board meeting out here about it, Mr Haile and all the rest of them. Father, like myself, he told them straight: they wouldn't stop him and he was *going to cut the bank*. So he did. He cut it out here with Uncle Sam Winchester. Sam used the ditch crook, the pulling crook, Father was in his waders, and away it went. It didn't wash too much because after you got so far down, it was clay, it was hard as buggery.

'Now it only went so much because the river was still high. And my father used to say, "There's only one way for the water to go. Go across the other side of the river and cut it there!" We knew exactly where to go, mind. So did I. "And we'll drown Bridgwater out." They used to patrol the banks the other side with guns, night and day, because they were afraid we were going over to cut it. It would have gone right to Bridgwater. We'd have let the water go in half an hour, *just* like that. Cut the other side first, drain the Parrett and then let it out this side. It was only eighteen inches wide in they days. They thickened it afterwards.

'Father's brother, he was a farmer, Uncle Bill Hembrow. He was patrolling on the far side. There was four of them down there on Stanmoor Bridge in case we went down that way. Two going up and two going down all day and night. There used to be about a dozen of them. Come night-time, Uncle Sam Winchester said, "Well, let's wake 'em up. Get that old gun down and go down on the bank and fire two up into the air and then you'll see them up and down like rabbits" – as if we were going over to do it. We used to have a boat tied up out here and shout across to them: "Look, *we've* got the barge! *We've* got the shovels! *We've* got the spades! You won't stop us!" It was bloody marvellous.

'But we never did cut it. You couldn't with the farmers over there, could you, with the shotguns? They had the

On the banks of the Brue below Glastonbury Tor, capped by the tower of St Michael's Church.

control of the place, didn't they? But it was all right for them. No water in their houses up in Stoke or Othery. In here, there was stink enough to kill 'ee. When the water started to go out, you could hardly bloody live here. There was a stink for months. Silt and shit all over the place. We didn't get nothing from insurance. And who had the charity help? Just the few big farmers. We got fuck all. No, we had a bit. They had a motorboat and it used to swing in here through the gates. We had hampers full of all sorts, clothes, food from Bristol. And they used to take endless bloody photos of the "Poor Withy Growers of Athelney". It made the papers, didn't it, boosted the circulation, really set them up. But *we* didn't mind. People was used to it. And you know, Adam, what fucking fun, wasn't it?'

The sea-floods are different, more sudden, more alien, like a retribution. There is no warning. A sudden veering of the wind or a drop in pressure – a one-inch fall on the barometer can raise the sea by a foot – and 'Sinne overflowes our soules', as one pamphleteer wrote after the great inundation of the Levels in 1607. 'The Seas of all strange impieties have rusht in upon us: we are covered with the waves of abhomination and uncleannes: we are drowned in the black puddles of iniquity: wee swim up to the throates, nay even above the chins in Covetousnes.' The sea-surge, which had invaded the Levels at nine o'clock on a Tuesday morning, 20 January – 'the sunne being most fayrely and brightly spred' – was God's punishment and Somerset was without a Noah. One infant was seen in a strong wooden cradle, floating safely on the waves, but the others, the less innocent, suffered. 'Listen then how He menaceth,' the anonymous pamphleteer crooned, 'and stand amazed at the wonders of his wrath.' Men deserted their families to save themselves. Pigs floated, feeding, for a while on ricks and then fell off to drown. A shepherd up a tree saw his flock sink in front of him. Rabbits clung to sheep's backs until the wool became heavy with water and the sheep rolled over to drown. Whole houses were lifted off the earth where they stood and floated up and down like ships half sunk. A man of property found his 'deer wife and deerest children, presented to him by the tyrannous stream' all dead, and then soon after, as some real consolation, the box full of the deeds to his lands, tied to a rafter. Glastonbury Tor was an island. People sat 'inviron'd with death, miserably pouring out teares to increase ye waters which were already too aboundant . . . Thus Reader dost thou behold the wounds of thy bleeding Countrie.'

It is a scene all too easily reimagined today in the news broadcasts from the Ganges delta where, in 1985, tidal waves destroyed the pitiable shacks and fragile sea-walls thrown up by the people trying to live there. The condition of life cannot be very different from the Somerset Levels in 1607.

The moral geography of Jacobean England had shifted, in Somerset at least, by the night of 13 December 1981, when the same thing on a lesser scale happened again. There was a blizzard, the diesel had turned to jelly in the tanks of lorries and a Force Ten storm was blowing. The first power failures came just after 1 pm, 'peak-time', as the *Burnham on Sea and Highbridge Gazette and Express* reported, 'for the weekly Sunday lunch. Even those cooking with gas were badly hit if they had electric-drive spits or depended on the clock timer.'

A 25-foot tide was expected that evening but the south-westerly storm had pushed another 8 feet of water up into the Bristol Channel. A fat slab of water 8 feet thick and 10 miles square. As the tide peaked, the wind suddenly backed north-westerly, trapping the block of sea against the Somerset coast. There was no escape and between Porlock and Clevedon it breached the sea-wall in fifteen places. The surge drove up the Parrett and punched a hole the size of a dining-room in the bank at Moorland. The flower gardens in Burnham with their miniature walls were utterly devastated. The floral clock was unrecognisable. Clots of seaweed and other flotsam were seen drifting down Berrow Road. Sand was spotted swirling by the junction of Manor Gardens. Mr Frank Rogers of Winchester Road was blown sideways with two friends and said later: 'There were three instant religious converts that night. There was a big whoomph.' The electrics shorted in flooded cars and all over the country headlamps shone underwater and windscreen wipers wiped flooded screens until, with the batteries, they faded. In Morris Ingram's eel-farm at Hinkley Point, under the luminous shadow of the nuclear power station there, the water burst up through the floor of the office and turned over the fibre-glass tanks in which eels were living, releasing them to the sea.

Mayor Sibyl K. Norris of Burnham expressed fears that the EEC disaster fund had already been emptied by the Italian earthquake, but nevertheless sent her very best wishes to all the people of the town. Mr Tom King, the politician, took time off from his busy schedule to inspect the damage. The Reverend Michael Stagg said the young married couple from Nazareth had to do with makeshift arrangements at this time of year, too. Over 750 houses were flooded in Burnham and the owner of a department store said, anonymously, that, to be reasonable, this was, of course, good for business. An appeal was opened, strictly for cash, 'which, in the past, has been found to be more useful than goods'.

The worst breach was south of Burnham where about 700 yards of the sea defences were demolished. Between five and six thousand acres of farmland had gone under. Harold Reason of Stretcholt near Pawlett lost all but two of his 1,200 pigs. A heartbroken Mr Reason said: 'I have lost absolutely everything. Most of these pigs were only twelve hours away from going to slaughter. They'll have to go into fertiliser now.' On the roads there was a carpet of animal refugees – rats, rabbits and squirrels – so thick that cars could not help but squash them.

Mr Reason's neighbour, Bob Thorne, is a fisherman. He keeps 200 willow butts fixed to the river bed near Stretcholt. They are intended to catch salmon on the dropping tide but nowadays collect more of the rubbish – televisions, dismembered coffee tables – that swings in and out on the tide from Burnham and Bridgwater than fish from the sea. He has spent his life on the estuary of the Parrett. 'This was the first tidal wave we had. As it come up, it come in over about eight feet deep. And kept

running. If it had only been the *wave* that had come in over, and stopped behind him – just the wave – it would have been all right. But as the wave went on, the sea was building up behind him, like. As he was going along, it was still coming eight foot deep, *ten* mile behind him, till he run out up at Combwich.

'When it came in here, it just – *whouff* – you can see that new door, it hit that door straight down. I was up on the hill. As soon as the tidal wave hit, one of the farmers came round with his tractor, running away from it. He could see the depth of it in this house, so: Bang, bang on the bloody door up there. "Bob," he said, "quick. That bank's bust. Everything's gone." So I whipped on my coat. When we got halfway down the hill we met water and by the time we got to the front gate, the lights on the tractor were shining away under it. I walked into my house with it up to *here*! With bloody waders on!

'The sea-level's level, see, with the front bedroom windowsill at springs. And it was in here eight hours. All the furniture was all a buggery. Some of it went out the door and was gone. I got £200 to put the piano right. But I wasn't going to have him done. So I put a bit of polish on him and left him there for a bit of furniture. That money's still in the bank.

'There was dead pigs everywhere. I had sheep float in here. There were dead pigs scattered all up against the buildings. Cows could stand up above it. One man tried to claim that he had seventeen young heifers washed away, but they smelled a rat. Somebody slipped up and said something and that was that. I could tell you about a family that put a hosepipe all over the inside of the house and got a new lot of carpets out of it. You could say it was some sort of a bonanza round here.

'So after I'd been in the house to see it was all all right, I went straight out and went round. I had eight ewes but I couldn't see them. It was black as tar. I thought, "They've bloody gone. Eight ewes!" Then I heard *maaa* and thought "That come over in the corner," and there was one in the top of the hedge and all their legs – it was the legs in the top of the hedge that was holding them there. Looking along I could see seven heads, just heads out of the

Bob Thorne with his salmon butts at Black Rock near Stretcholt on
the estuary of the Parrett. Only butts made of willow can take the
strain of the tides without buckling.

Arthur and Mabel Stuckey at home near Langport. 'There have been several drowned here . . .'

water. So I stuck there with them all night. They was all in lamb and they all had their lambs two months later. The other one we never found her. She went on down towards the A38 somewhere.

'The garden still ain't right now from the salt. Things don't grow like it used to. We had an aeroplane over here, chucking little brown balls from the helicopter. It was coming down like bloody rain. It didn't do no bloody good. It was coming in here with the bloody bucket swung on for four or five days. Grass'll stick the salt. It won't hurt the grass, but growing ground's different. And it ain't growing.'

These are rare moments. But if 'the forces that produce the branch angles of the oak lie potent in the acorn', there is always the threat of water in the presence of a wetland. It is a double, subtle landscape poised between certainties. The private threat of water takes the form of drowning. Harold Hembrow's sister drowned in the Tone. 'She got up on the bank in the winter time, clambered up over the steps. Mother thought she was out doing something. She ran out and she couldn't find her. She didn't know where she was to. She was in the river for three months before she was found. That was the way of it. That was Mary. It isn't any good worrying over it. I don't.'

Arthur and Mabel Stuckey live in a lock-keeper's cottage on the Parrett just below Langport. They have been married sixty years. (*Arthur*: I'll tell you how we met. She was standing on the doorstep in Bow Street. I was going out there to a football match. I looked across the road at her. She said: 'Where are you going?' I said: 'Going out to a football match. Coming?' She said 'yes' and off we went.) In that time they have seen a string of drownings.

Arthur: My brother-in-law drowned in the river. He used to pole two planks around the moor in the winter. It was just by the little pumphouse up the top. It was a very rough night. We never knew what happened, how he got in there. We picked him out of the locks at the end. 1933 that was. George Brooks.

Mabel: Not many of them have drowned accidentally. A lot of them have jumped in over. We saw an old woman jumping off the bridge. An old gypsy woman – that was before we were married. Peppermint Lil, wasn't it?

Arthur: She didn't jump off. She just sat on the bridge and tumbled back over. Now I wouldn't be surprised if she was drunk when she did it.

Mabel: The solicitor's wife, she drowned herself there – and her daughter – and there was a schoolteacher drowned herself here, and there was an old tramp. He come up the bank one night and *walked* in. Instead of turning the bend like that, he walked straight on towards the light in the middle of the bridge and got drowned in the river. They pulled him out down here behind the doors.

Arthur: That woman from Somerton, she got drowned.

Mabel: There have been several drowned here. Most of them washed up in the locks. We wouldn't touch them. The police would hook them out. They found one of them down at Burnham-on-Sea. She must have gone over two weirs, here and at Oath. The water used to flow faster in they days.

Harold Hembrow: Oh yes, they've ruined everything. They've made a mess of it, haven't they?

Floods are rarer now. The December sea-surge in 1981 is unlikely to happen again within the next 250 years. Nevertheless, the sea-level is rising at 2.5 millimetres, or a tenth of an inch, a year and the defences have been raised and strengthened. Inland, on the moors, the drainage system has been all but perfected, with new pumping stations and enough capacity in the channels to absorb all but the heaviest flows during tide-lock. The cutting of the Huntspill River in the Levels north of the Poldens during the war virtually solved the problems of flooding there, while in the southern Levels another great flood in the Tone valley in 1960, when Taunton itself was badly affected and the water came over the top of the radiators of the buses in the Western National depot, provided the impetus for expensive new drainage works.

Electric pumping stations were installed on the moors

Willows that were once pollarded every few years near Sharpham have been left to grow to their natural height. The trunks lean and split under the extra weight and will eventually collapse.

south of Langport. The banks of the Tone, the Parrett, and of the Isle and the Yeo, its tributaries, have been fortified. The King's Sedgemoor Drain has been widened and deepened and the Parrett basin joined to it by means of another new river, the Sowy. Now, whenever there is too much water in the Parrett, it will simply slop over into the Sowy and run away into the King's Sedgemoor Drain. The big pumps that line the Parrett were previously able to work only if the river itself was not too high. Now they can dry a moor virtually at will.

Wallace Musgrave of Burrow Bridge has been a drainage man all his life and sees himself as the heir to all the drainage works since the thirteenth century. His brother began before him and was the Curry Moor pump man for thirty-four years, but as Wallace says, 'I've eclipsed him now with all this drainage. He's eclipsed for good, in fact. He's gone on.' Wallace is the pillar of the Baptist Chapel in Burrow Bridge and is full of the sparkling non-conformist irreverence for worldly authority. He came out of school in 1926. 'It was depressed then. You were held down. You had Thatcherism about ten times more intensive and cruel than it is today. You couldn't move. A man was kept in place.'

The Musgrave family lived on the banks of the Tone in Athelney and the flood in 1929 forced them upstairs for six weeks. 'We had a boat and we had windows large enough outside with a ladder to be able to get in and out, so we stayed. There was an oil fire for cooking upstairs, but we had to fetch our water from a well in Athelney farm. The mains busted, but that wasn't anything very spectacular. The water always used to be turned off for a day or two. Nobody knew why. It first came through pipes up there in 1911. Before that, they had to have river water. It had to be boiled, though.

'In 1911, which was one of the hottest summers we have ever had, so I've been told, diphtheria was quite frequent. You look in any of the churchyards here, you see the little kids of so many months – sometimes there's half a dozen on some of the tombstones. A distant relative of mine, one of the underdogs that had got up amongst the councillors and so on – he'd chickened up to oppose a colonel in North Curry for a seat and had got on to the Taunton Board of Guardians – he created hell. He'd lost one girl himself. They'd been trying to get piped water for years. It was like trying to get blood out of a stone. He went to town about this and eventually the supply came through. But before that, it was river water. Now in the winter it was all right. Flood water was a little better than what it was in the summer. In a dry summer, it would be terrible. But the river's tidal and mud would flow up through. You'd have to catch the tide when it was out – you only had a few hours, see – and then you would dip the water carefully. My mother would put it in great earthenware pans on the table with three or four other great pans and they would transfer it from one to the other after it settled for an hour and that was that. There would be sediment settled down in the bottom of each of them. And then finally it was a little clearer and she would boil it. After that, you could say it was beautiful. But that's all the water they had before 1911.'

In 1934, Wallace Musgrave got the job of driving the steam engine in the Aller Moor pumping station at Burrow Bridge. It had been built there in 1869 across the old bed of the Cary, which the monks of Glastonbury had channelled away from King's Sedgemoor in the thirteenth century to bring it down into the Parrett at Burrow Bridge. He explains: 'The abbots were the great tin gods of the area. They could do what they liked and they did more good up to the time of the River Board Commissioners

Wallace Musgrave in the pumping station at Burrow Bridge. 'As it happens I was the first dirty-booted, uneducated, humble fellow that was appointed to the job of expenditor. Apparently they thought there was a little soil under the scalp up here that was worth cultivating.'

Southlake Moor is still deliberately flooded in the winter to allow
the thick silty water from the Parrett to feed the land. The rhynes
and ditches are marked out by the low ridges on each bank, the
accumulation of the silt and plants pulled out of them over many
years. In the background the low island of 'Sowy' rises above
the moor.

Julian Honeybun, a farmer's son from outside Meare, wildfowling on the moor. The winter floods attract large numbers of ducks and waders and one or two farmers to shoot them.

coming in than all the others in the area. Now one of these rascals, one of these vicars or parsons or bishops, organised men to drain King's Sedgemoor. They had the varnish of some religious order on them but, as regards their sincerity, I shouldn't think it went very deep. Now then, ten thousand years ago, or whatever, everything used to shoot right out all over the wild places by Moorlinch and then the whole lot had to trickle back down out here somehow. Everything in Aller Moor, everything in King's Sedgemoor, including the River Cary, whether it was downfall or spillwater, there was no way it could get into the estuary. Now then, what happened to the water? Where did it go? It didn't shoot up over the Polden Hills or come on over Westonzoyland Aerodrome or anything of that. That land was twenty, thirty, forty feet higher than the land in the moors. The water *had* to come back and it used to run willy-nilly, flood Earlake and God knows what. Now then, the abbots of these monasteries, principally by the means of barriers rather than drains, did an enormous amount of work. Instead of letting the River Cary run all about King's Sedgemoor, they sent it down by the A372 along Beer Wall, cutting it off from King's Sedgemoor, and then sending it down the A361 with the Burrow Wall.

'They didn't do a bad job. They saved King's Sedgemoor from all that Cary water, but it was probably too much for the Parrett, with the Tone coming in here too. So in 1790 they had a better idea. Why not drain King's Sedgemoor with its own drain straight out to the Parrett at Dunball? So in 1790, they had a pilot King's Sedgemoor Channel cut. And it was pretty good. There were some big timbers in there when we widened it in 1938, and they hadn't done a bad job at all. We had to shift those timbers with excavators.

'Now then, when it came to draining Aller Moor, the high and mighty farmers on the Aller Moor Drainage Board consulted Mr Easton and he proposed in 1869 to use the old disused bed of the Cary, cut by the monks those very many years ago, and put the pumping station right on the spot where it joined the Parrett. He had the channel cleaned out, the culverts put right and the pump put in. Now the pump is a good two miles down the channel from the nearest part of Aller Moor, so Mr Easton made a wise choice. The gravitation is excellent. I had the privilege of driving this engine for the last twenty-one years of its life from 1934 to 1955. The job was to pump "Whenever required" – that is to say: Keep the water *off* the moor. Sometimes there would be no pumping at all between April and October. And then in the winter I might be pumping seven or eight hours a day, with the chimney belching black smoke and steam puffing out from morning to night.'

In 1955, the River Authority cut a new rhyne joining Aller Moor to the King's Sedgemoor system and the pump into the Parrett at Burrow Bridge became redundant. It is now, as Wallace says, 'resplendent as a museum piece'. Like a few other steam pumps on the Levels, it sits immobile in its brick house, shiny, perfectly balanced, unused in a permanent summer. As for the thirteenth-century bed of the Cary, one of the first proper drainage works in the Levels, still rimming the edge of Southlake Moor, fringed in irises and paved with lily pads, Wallace comments, 'Now it's only a tiddly bit of a ditch.'

The closure of the Burrow Bridge pumping station and the forgetting of the Cary was not the end of Musgrave's career in drainage. He had already become expenditor to the Aller Moor Drainage Board, the one professional employed by the farmers and landowners in each district to supervise the drainage of their land. 'If you employ a doctor, you've got to do what he tells you to and, to some extent, I suppose, I'm a physician. Now then, most of the expenditors were pompous fellows – you would think they were General de Gaulle or Winston Churchill or something – the sort of man who thought he could sharpen a pencil better than the others. And as it happens I was the first dirty-booted, uneducated, humble fellow that was appointed to the job of expenditor. Apparently they thought there was a little soil under the scalp up here that was worth cultivating.' He had made the transition, rare enough in this structured society, from controlled to controller, from the Hembrows' impotent shouting, 'We've got the barge, we've got the shovels' to the man in charge of the banks and sluices himself. He is known in Burrow Bridge as 'long-headed', and eventually rose to become the supervisor of all the labour on the drainage works in the Parrett valley in the last twenty years or so, which have ensured that 1929 will never happen again.

'Don't be so sure. The Lord sends about the average rainfall, thank goodness for us, year by year. He sends it sometimes in bigger gobs than others. Sometimes he sprinkles it about. All right. Sometimes it comes a little hasty. Now in all my lifetime as a drainage man, every peak flood exceeds the previous. Why's that? It's simple. Use your loaf. Our catchment goes into Dorset, hilly country as you get up off. There's improvements made up there. There's impervious surfaces – glass, concrete, tarmac. Drains you put in. Roads go down. Impervious. Let's have a whole new housing estate on that hillside! Lovely! And where's it going? It's all going to be coming to Burrow Bridge. And of course it's speeding up. In the old days, when the barges were running, men had two days to get their loads ready, either to go to Ham or what have you, when there'd be more water to get them up there. They'd say: "Rain today, Tuesday. It'd be Friday morning before we'd have to be away." But if it started raining now at midday, before I go to bed tonight, what fetched up Yeovil would be going under Burrow Bridge. Oh no, it comes like billy-o, and there'll be another big flood yet and you won't know the difference between now and a thousand years ago.'

Water and the controlling of water has made the landscape of the Levels. Water under control is the life of the place. Each of the moors, each hydrologically separate patch with its different flows and different demands, has its own Internal Drainage Board, an oligarchy of the farmers with over twenty acres who decide the levels and clean the rhynes. Water is not an evil to be banished but a presence to be made use of. There is, for example, the crucial difference between downfall and spillwater. Rainwater – downfall – is sterile, acid and empty, chilling the ground, delaying growth and spoiling the fields. But spillwater – thick water, as it is called – has come down the rivers, full of the silts and goodness from upstream, rich with the muck that has washed off the roads and yards into the drains, invisibly thickened with the fertilisers and nutrients farmers have put on their land 'up off'. It is the best manure there is, settling down and out on the moors, quite literally thickening them, a liquid topsoil, so that on either side of some of the older banks (there is a graphic example near Combe just north of Langport) where the floods have been held back in deliberate washlands, there is a three-foot difference in ground level, three foot of Dorset goodness spread out over a Somerset meadow.

The deliberate flooding of the moors with spillwater is still done in some places, on Southlake Moor near Burrow Bridge for example. It has also acted in the past as a form of pest control, drowning unwanted bugs. Those that managed to climb up the gate-posts would be visited in boats and burnt with a paraffin rag. It is also said that the weight of water in a flood smooths out the surface of the fields so that afterwards there is no need to roll them. It is undoubtedly true that a field is flatter after a flood – even molehills disappear – but calculations of the pressures involved have shown that the weight of water even in the deepest flood is not enough to flatten the field. It may be that the peculiar jelly-like quality of the peat – its absorbency – adjusts in the presence of water, settling out into flatness as the most viscous of soups.

A flood also provides habitats for wildfowl and in the past could spare overworked horses. Hay used to be put in ricks in the summer on little high spots near the meadow from which it was cut and then, come the winter floods, would be collected by boat – infinitely more fluent than the sticky process of hauling it out by horse and cart.

Water is a curse turned gift. In the summer, between May and September, when the cows can get out on to the moorland fields, the rhynes and ditches which are used to evacuate the winter rains have water penned up in them to provide wet fences between the fields and ready drinking water for the animals. These summer rhynes,

The rhynes are the ever-present frontiers in the Levels, dividing
worlds, separating stock, and marking out the territory.

Harold Hembrow and Charlie Keirle clear a ditch next to a withy bed on West Sedgemoor.

On Tealham Moor, which is still one of the wettest parts of the Levels, the waxy yellow flowers of Marsh Marigold gild the margins of a rhyne. This intimate between-world, neither entirely land nor entirely water, is the core of a wetland.

The cabbagy leaves of Butterbur on Shapwick Heath in the lush damp of the peatlands north of the Poldens.

hidden at first as you stare out across the endless and apparently undivided grass, with only odd, arbitrary gates sticking up in the flatness, is where the wetness of the moors concentrates. It is as though the grass were no more than skin, a tightened membrane over the body of water, and these rhynes, incised in that skin with all the precision of improving surgery, had cut through to the substance of the place itself. Each shelters a particular world of butterbur or kingcup, of water mint or a great wedding-show of irises. There is a must in the air above the peaty waters. On either side, there is the dazed flitting of the Minton blue damselflies and the haze of the meadow grasses, both part of the one summer thickness, folding into each other, making an insect haze and a grass hum.

If you sit on the banks of one of these rhynes, the high water in the field soaks up into the cloth of your trousers, so that the only thing to do is swim and move over from the watery peat to the peaty water, a half-noticed change from one half-element to another. There is no need to step into the rhyne. Simply stand in the shallow margin of the water, next to the water-mint and the sweet violet, and let your feet slide down over the warm skin of the peat below you. Slowly the body lowers into the cider-soup, crusty with frog-bit and duckweed, with seeds and reed-shells. The points of the arrowhead quiver in your slight wash and, away down the rhyne, the slimed light bodies of the secret eels release a bubble each as they shift away from the strange disturbance. The breadth of the rhyne grows as you come near the surface to a generous, private, pacific width, lobed into by the irises and reeds. The peat must is heady from the broken water and a swan claps in another field. The meadow is riffled in the wind. Heat and vapour wobble in the air above it. The still water is slick on the skin. Nothing is dissolved in it. Everything hangs there in suspension. Time stops. Your body is a golden unnatural brown seen through the whisky water. You hang embedded in the place as though in a tomb, with some strange osmosis of the water sliding into the heart through the skin. It is a soggy, ambivalent fringe world, a world hinged to *both* and *and*. A thousand million years ago, all life was water-life and to float in the semi-substance of a summer rhyne is to return to that antiquity.

But do not be discovered or admit to this odd behaviour. Floating in the rhynes is not what the moor-men do themselves and they will lecture you on the dangers of fluke and other diseases. If you live in a place, some distance must be preserved.

The Levels are as sensitive as cricket to the weather. If it were a wet summer, there would be acres of moorland which would go untouched. As Dick House, a farmer in Stoke St Gregory and Chairman of the West Sedgemoor Drainage Board, says: 'It wasn't a proper life in a bad year. It was slavery. You just didn't pay people in a wet year. Everything was turned off. The difference between a good year and a bad year was the difference between sinking and survival. You sank in the wet; you survived in the dry. It was a vicious circle. If it was a wet year, people on the high ground had all the hay they wanted and you couldn't get on to the moor to get your own off at all. That would be a terrific, a terrible bad time. In 1929, the summer was wet and the price of West Sedgemoor hay, which was usually chaffed-up and sent by rail to feed pit ponies in Wales, sank to 15 shillings a ton. But now when it was a dry year, things were very different. Everyone up off would be short of hay, and weren't we all delighted? Down there on the moor, it would be growing away like nobody's business. So in 1919, a very dry summer, West Sedgemoor hay was selling at £12.10.0 a ton. What, seventeen times what it was worth in a bad year. Four new houses were built out of that hay on West Sedgemoor that year. It's the most productive land in England if only it's dry.'

Arrowhead is one of the later colonisers, pushing up through the frogbit and rooted in the floor of the rhyne.

Gathering hay on Queen's Sedgemoor.

Dry, of course, is a relative term and the dependable growth of hay on the 'plump-thigh'd moor and full-flanck't marsh' as Michael Drayton described them in 1613 meant that the grass on the Levels has always been a valuable resource. Coastal villages and up-country parishes maintained rights to graze animals on these summer pastures well into the nineteenth century, while there are records of cattle from Gloucestershire, Devon, Dorset and even Ireland being brought to graze on Sedgemoor in a dry year.

The water, apart from feeding the grasses, bears another fruit: the fish. Mabel Stuckey: 'You could always see the carp lying on the water sunning themselves. When the water was a nice height and the sun was shining down, you could see the carp all laid out, on top of the water, sunning themselves. What a beautiful picture. We used to gut them, split them down, put them in the pig salter, hang them on the beam, let them dry. When we got short of grub, we'd wash all the salt out of them, stuff them with sage and onion, cook them in a deep dish with fat in them. You never tasted anything so nice.'

But even the fat lolling carp, or the salmon that Mabel Stucky can remember jumping at the weir on the Parrett below Langport bridge, lack the real moorland élan – the mud-hugging, depth-seeking allure of the eel. The Levels are an eely place. These one-fin fish, the fin swept along from neck to tail and back along the belly, are secret and discreet. They seep into all the tiny capillaries of the moors, with none of the terminal drive of the salmon or the lamprey, which boringly insist on pushing on up the main current towards the source to breed. Instead, the eel infiltrates its living quarters at any point, slip-seeking any hidden overhang, any dark obsessive pool, any ditch or sunken rhyne, where in weed or under stones it can feel the touch of solid, moory substance close around its skin. Eels are *thigmotic*, that is: they love to touch, not to roam in any pike-like abstraction, but to slide down into the bottom-stuff of ditches and rivers.

So hungry are they for cover, for this touch, that one can catch an eel simply by putting a sack full of straw on the river-bed, with a length of drain embedded in it. Leave the sack overnight, which is when eels move, and with no bait and no entrapment, one of them will be laid up there in the morning. Fishermen who catch eels (usually in fyke nets where entry but no exit is possible) store them in tanks before sending them to market. If a length of drainpipe is left in the tank, the eels will crowd into it, slipped in there as tightly as the coils of gut inside the stomach wall, their own bodies, easily – one wants to say *affectionately* – slid up against the others in the cylinder, so that if you pick it up and tip it, a sliding clotted mass of them, folded together as though of one piece, will flop out as a sort of solid liquid into the water. The embodiments of touch, of sinuous fluency, each eel a map of a river shifting over time, these *addicts* of touch with all their dense sociability, their tactile sensuality, these are the real spirits of the Levels.

Put them in a bucket and they do not slither noiselessly over each other as you would expect. They are too mundane for that; there is nothing abstract about the eel. Out of the bucket instead comes a soft tactile gossip from their bodies, the rasp of liquid kissing. Or, according to Michael Brown, the eel man from Thorney: the noise of sex on a hot afternoon.

In the medieval economy of the moors, when they were still, according to a seventeenth-century improver, 'so corse, level and subjecte to waters by raine and surroundinge streams, and thereby so cold, heartless and barren that it affordeth not, in muche of it, the twentieth part of the fruit it would thankfully yield . . .', the double resource of land and water was seen in a more positive light. It was the combination of land and water which had drawn Stone Age people here in the first place.

Apart from the summer pasture and the alder and willow timber to be taken off the fen woodland, the moor provided fish. And above all other fish, it provided eels. In the Domesday Book, eels appear as a sort of moorland

currency. A garden in Langport was rented out at sixty eels a year. Two fisheries belonging to the Benedictine Abbey at Muchelney were worth 6,000. The accounts of the abbey at Glastonbury include a fishery at Middlezoy, one at Andredesey (2,000 eels), at Clewer (7,000), at Martinsey on the Axe (another 7,000) and one at Othery, run by Wlgar, which paid the abbey 3,000 eels a year and seventeen pence. Alfred's abbey at Athelney took 6,000 eels from the moorland waters every year, 1,000 of them from a fishery at Stathe.

The abbeys built weirs across the rivers to pen back the water into pools where the fish could be netted. This led to conflict – the archetypal conflict of the Levels – between those whose interest was in the water for its fish and those with an interest in the land, for its pasture and even arable crops. There are endless records of farmers in the Middle Ages breaking down the monastic weirs – there was one across the Parrett just below Burrow Mump – and of violent feuds between the abbeys themselves over conflicting rights to parts of the Levels and conflicting ideas of the way they were to be managed. The Deans of Wells and the Abbots of Glastonbury maintained a vendetta throughout the thirteenth century over weirs on the River Brue, while west of the Parrett near Burrow Bridge it was the Abbot of Athelney – a far lesser tin god – with whom Wells came into conflict. Their major dispute over the future of Stanmoor was settled in 1250 when the Abbot met the Dean, like Napoleon and Alexander at Tilsit, in the middle of the moor itself, a few yards from the site of Harold Hembrow's house. The Abbot of Athelney was forced to concede all rights to the moor, including the eels, except for the collection of firewood.

The eel is at one extreme, the heron at the other, with the Levels strung between them. Zoologists call eels benthic, meaning they are not free-floaters but live down in the depths of their chosen water. The eel is perfect, in its sheen of efficiency, its introversion, scarcely distinct from the place it makes its own, like a cancer, spread into every cell of the moors. And the heron is public, bedraggled, alert (nothing could ever bedraggle an eel), standing on the edge of a rhyne with all the electric, neurotic poise of a man waiting to bid and careless of his appearance; or then clumsying away from one water to the next, its legs straggled out behind, its head zigzagged back into an awkward body. Nothing is more incongruous, more unlikely than a heron, no more than the mechanical sketch of a fish-catching bird with the parts somehow bolted together. And nothing more congruous than the eel. It is animal made chic. The eel and the heron, the effortless and the vigilant, the langorous and the taut, the heart and mind of a wetland.

I have seen a heron catch an eel only once. I had imagined that it would be a sort of culmination, as one form of the Levels disappeared down the gullet of another. but it ended up nothing of the kind. There was no climax in the act. The heron stood on the bank of the Langacre Rhyne on King's Sedgemoor looking spare. Some distance away, a man was swinging at the bankside growth with a ditch-hook. Two motorbikes went off down the Beer Wall, slewing on the thirteenth-century bends as the heron struck. It was no more than a licked finger flicking over the last note in a bundle of fives and the eel was out on the bank, an ignominious wriggle. All grace had gone and that liquid pouring of the one curve travelling the muscles of its back was forgotten in the horrible ignobility of being eaten. The heron jumped sideways as if away from a fire, jerked the eel around in its mouth and, in glutinous stages, swallowed it. The bird looked shocked, stared sideways and then bounced into flight with a spring at its elbow-knees to flap off back to some tree-top nest. That was that. As flat as that. The

Part of Brendan Sellick's catch from Bridgwater Bay. 'The slimed, light bodies of the secret eels . . .'

bikes came back down the Beer Wall and the man cleaning the ditch moved over to the other side.

If the eel's manner of death can be mundane, its birth and early life are nothing short of extraordinary. About 130 million years ago, when the Atlantic was no more than the Bristol Channel, when Delaware nudged up against Devon and most of the world was covered by the Pacific, the ancestors of the European eel, *Anguilla anguilla*, spawned a few miles out in this narrow sea and the young eels came inland to live and feed off the richer freshwater streams. This was the simple pattern: birth at sea, life inland, with a single short journey each way at the beginning and at the end. But the world shifted under the eel. Convection in the rocks of the earth's mantle pushed Europe and America apart, a fraction of an inch a year. Meanwhile, the eel stayed faithful to its old pattern, leaving the Parrett – or its ancestor – as a mature fish, swimming to the increasingly distant birth grounds and then returning as a larva the shape of a willow leaf, washed back to Europe on the currents of the Gulf Stream. This cycle, once no more than a few miles each way, now stretches the width of the Atlantic.

The eel which the heron picked out of the Langacre Rhyne had begun life 4,000 miles away in the Sargasso Sea, 300 miles south-west of Bermuda, maybe eight years before, in March, a hundred fathoms below the surface of the ocean. For three years, the willow-leaf larva had floated towards England until it arrived over the continental shelf and, somehow recognising the change in the seabed in a process still not understood, had metamorphosed into a tiny transparent eel called an elver. From willow-leaf drifter, distributed by the currents anywhere between Norway and the Sea of Azov, the eel turns deliberate, able to swim against the current and equipped with the most extraordinary sense of smell in nature. Experiments on adult eels have shown that they can smell one part in three million million million, or a millilitre of rosewater (it was a German experiment) in a lake fifty-eight times the size of Lake Constance.

You must imagine this in the springtime all over Europe, at the mouths of rivers from the Dnieper to the Jakobselv and in Bridgwater Bay at the mouth of the Parrett, as the indescribable mass of glass-eels gather at the estuaries to move inland. The numbers are incalculable but it is known that each female eel in the Sargasso Sea lays between five and ten million eggs. The elver horde smells the fresh water from out at sea and begins to swim in towards it. They sink away from light at ebb tide as the water drops and only come up into the high water at flood. A thick harvest of them when high water coincides with the hours of darkness moves inland. This is the great springtime impregnation of the moors as the sperm mass of eel life pushes into the wetland, and this is when the people are waiting for them.

The elvers ride the night tide. All along the banks of the Parrett, from Bridgwater up to Oath Lock, and on the Tone from Burrow Bridge up into Curry Moor, fishermen wait with their elver nets, giant scoops like the shovels in sweet shops with which the humbugs are dug out of jars. The frame is willow or aluminium, the net itself a fine nylon cheesecloth. There is competition for places on the bank and the fishermen are there hours before the flood. The elver brokers set up receiving stations on the bank, with scales hanging from a floodlit tripod beside a van carrying tanks into which the elvers will be poured. Each station has its own team of catchers spread out along the river; these have been recruited in a long courtship of men who are naturally independent and mildly suspicious. The air is thick with conspiracy and expectation – in the darkness of it, the storm lanterns reflected in the river, the defence of the spot, the muttering of catchers pulled at by the breeze and the faint tinge of illegality. Elvers are driven by a hunger for land water and the best spots are where 'freshes' spring out into the main river. If you happen to know – or even *be* – someone who has the key to one of the pumping stations, which can push gallons of sweet-smelling moor water out into the river, then your chances of catching an elver will be greatly increased – as would, if they ever got to know about it, the anger of Wessex Water Authority.

A few years ago, the officers of the Inland Revenue came down to the river and started asking questions about the actual value of people's catches. This was, of course, very properly resented by the fishermen themselves and ever since the individual catches seem to have declined disastrously, none of them in fact coming up to the tax threshold, while the number of people who have decided, apparently, to take up elver-catching has shown a marked increase. Rumours that names and payments might even have been invented, or that one man's catch might have been marked down to ten fictitious characters from various villages, are rigorously denied.

Should you actually walk down the bank yourself as a stranger and ask what the fishing is like, you will certainly be told that it has never been quite so bad as that very night itself and that some terrible reluctance must have come over the entire elver population of the Atlantic Ocean. And where are you from anyway? But make a friend and go elver-catching with him and you will find yourself on the secret, earwig underworld of the elver. In the moonlight by the pumping station, the filthy tide with all the rubbish from Burnham is still sliding up. Dark silhouettes of gunge push on towards Taunton. The moonlight is a skin on the bankside slime and everything is ready: the two nets, the tin bath, the stack of trays on which elvers once caught must be spread if they are to be kept alive. Elvers can breath in air for several hours, but if kept in a bucket for too long they use up the oxygen in the water and die.

While the tide is running, the elvers stay with it in midstream. The first sign of dead water is a stillness at the bankside which gradually spreads in towards the middle of the river until there is no movement at all. Then the deep lick of the tide, like a lolling tongue into Somerset, starts to slide away and the elvers move into the banks where the outward flow is least. This is the moment. The electric pump is turned on and the artificial upswelling sends fresh warts of silver water out into the dropping Tone. The nets go in, held against the bank just downstream of the pump's own concrete outflow.

You might find nothing. The elver is capricious. If the day has been cold and there is no warmth in the mud, they might never move. But it might be the night in which the little glass-eels come streaming into the nets and are then poured out of them ('We've got one or two here') in twisting filaments of spun glass ('We've got a breakfast here') like the drooling juices from a cow's lips, into the tin bath. There the elvers weave a constant slimed rope in the torchlight, generating a sort of froth called vump. The sliding of each individual body matches the shape of the others' so that it is no confused mass but an organised wreath of them, scores thick, twisting up here and there into candle-flame points which peak and collapse to restore the continuity of the animated wave.

There are hundreds of elver stories invoking not lengths but numbers, hogsheads and bathfuls caught in one night. Fred Lock caught enough elvers one night to feed his ducks for ten weeks. Harold Durston once caught so many that he spread them over his garden as manure. And so on. Their traditional fate is in an omelette with a duck's egg – the sensation is of faintly marine spaghetti – but the quantities of elvers now caught in the Parrett and Tone have a different destination. As long ago as 1965, aeroplanes were flying English elvers from Gloucester to Poland. There are annual deliveries to Lake Balaton in Hungary. Until recently, they have been air-freighted live in ice-packed polystyrene boxes to Japanese fish-farms. Morris Ingram's eel farm at Hinkley Point takes several hundred kilos a year. Dutch and German merchants buy Somerset elvers to make up the shortfall from their own overfished and polluted rivers, but the most extraordinary trade in these extraordinary animals began in 1985.

Several tons of elvers, a mixture of those caught on the Parrett and the Severn, were transported live in cooled aerated tanks across the width of Europe to Minsk in Byelorussia. The Russians had demanded a veterinary certificate of health for the animals. A Taunton vet who had spent forty years looking up cows duly came out to the tanks, peered in at the infinite transparent threads,

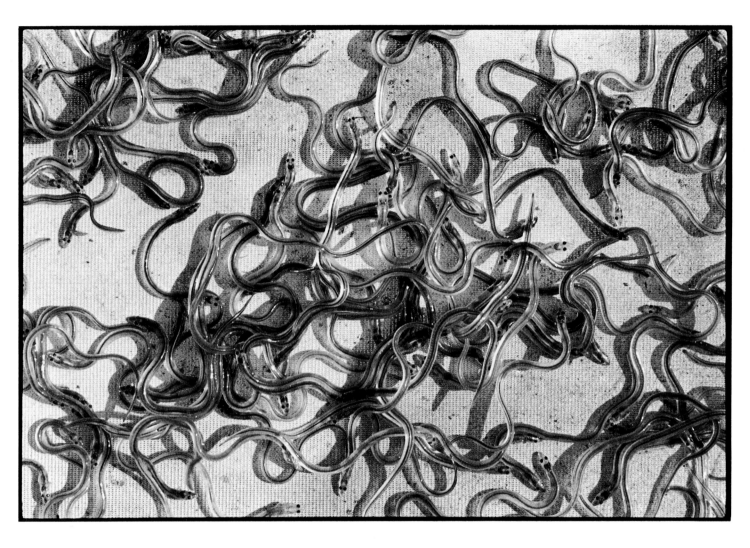

Elver fishermen on the River Parrett below Burrow Mump: taking
the annual harvest from the Atlantic.

Elvers on the nylon mesh of a fisherman's tray.

Jonathan Coate rayballing on the River Tone. A record of 86 eels in two hours.

pronounced them in peak condition and signed some flamboyant, stamped-on document. This was produced at the receiving station in Minsk. The vodka came out. Reflections were exchanged on Nato and the Warsaw Pact and then bucket after bucket of Somerset elvers were poured from the English lorry into a fleet of Russian trucks standing about in the Byelorussian frost. At length, the trucks set off for the east, to deliver the elvers to the Volga and the Ob', to the Jenisej and the Lena where, of course, the life in ditches or under the roots of a willow would be indistinguishable from Curry Moor or the Langacre Rhyne.

If the elvers escape the depredations of the fishermen, they will percolate out into the moor, become the thick life of it, its hidden, living intestines. Their bodies darken and, as they start to feed, turn a yellowy green. The young fingerling eels develop strange purple retinas which give them no more than a dusky, crepuscular vision of the world. Once they have come to their rhyne or river patch, they will move no more than a hundred yards or so from year to year. This is their limited world: laid up in the mud all winter, scarcely shifting, and then in the springtime, as the river grows warmer, starting to search for food, picking off young lampreys, sticklebacks, even trout and elvers, the larvae of insects, mussels, snails and, on newly flooded areas, drowned earthworms.

They do not gulp their prey but snatch at them with a wrench of their own bodies. It is this which allows the eel to be caught by the technique known as rayballing or clotting. Earthworms – rays – are tied to a long bit of wool which is bundled up into a ball and attached to a length of firm wire on the end of a pole. There is no hook. The rayball is held in the running water – the best weather is a heavy thunderstorm in May or June – and the smell of the worms courses off downstream. The eels come running and while clinging to the rayball, trying to wrench some of the worms away, are hoiked out of the water and held over a tin bath floating in the river where, in panic, they drop off and are caught. Jonathan Coate and a friend of his once caught eighty-six eels in two

hours with two clats and one tin bath on the Tone. Those without a tin bath can use an upside-down umbrella floating in the stream.

'A great big long pole with a great big bunch of worms on the end' (Mabel Stuckey's description) is not the only way. Eel traps made of green willow, stuffed in culverts and packed around with weed and stones, and fyke nets with wings and a long tail, all of them with cones in the throat where the eel can enter but not escape, catch them just as well. And there are spears:

Arthur Stuckey: Get in the nose of the boat, let the boat drift down and just push the spear into the mud. It would be a fifteen-foot long handle. A young larch would be used for the handle. You'd catch four or five at a time. They couldn't get out past the notches in the prongs, see. But it was banned after the war.

Mabel: You can't catch a fish now.

Harold Hembrow: Fifty quid an eel spear now! Tis all bloody money!

Arthur: My father used to have an eel trunk. It was a big box, two foot six square, six foot long, with a cover on there, all perforated, all drilled, made of oak. Drop it in the river with a big chain on, pull him up the bank, drop eels in there, push him back in and that's where they'd stay. Then they'd go up in barrels to London where the Jews wanted them. It was always the Jews that ate the eels. They used to go up on the trains from Langport station.

If the eel has survived elvering, clotting, trapping, netting and spearing by man or heron, it might live seven years or more in the rhyne before the last great metamorphosis. The back darkens, the belly silvers, the eyes grow larger and acquire a golden shimmer. The snout sharpens and, as the eel stops feeding, the gut shrinks away. The eel is now mature and these are preparations for the sea, for the 4,000-mile return journey to the birth-ground. The

Michael Brown loading his eel smoker in Drayton.

Fred Lock strips the skin from an eel 'like rolling the stocking off a girl's leg'.

time of migration begins in October, as the water starts to cool, and continues throughout the winter.

But it is no dribble of fish out from the land to the sea. Many conditions have to be satisfied before the silver eel will run and there may only be three or four nights in the whole winter on which those conditions hold. The eels are great romantics: the night must be dark, at some time between sunset and midnight, between the last and first quarters of the moon; it must be wild and stormy, best if there is a deep low over the Channel and a fierce easterly blowing the land water out to sea; the river must be brimful with dirty thick flood water, impenetrable with the silt in it and the tide must have been a good deep one, pushing the smell of salt far into the moors. Then and only then will the silvers go. It is the autumn equivalent of the elver nights in the spring and if the elvers are the moment of conception, the seeding of the Levels, the thundery wildness of the night of the silver run is a sort of birth. Now the moors deliver up their fruit that has been gestating seven, ten or even fifteen years, as secretly in the place as in a womb.

On the silver night, the eels emerge, make one great display and go. Bob Thorne, the fisherman from Stretcholt, was out walking one night at the beginning of November a year or so ago. 'It was blowing and raining. I was going out to fish the shrimp nets. It must have been near midnight. It was blowing a good gale and pouring. I could hear this rustling beside the wind, all around me. I shone my torch about and the ground was alive with eels making for the main watercourse, over by the bay next to Corner Island. I should imagine they were coming out of the pits and ditches. They were travelling at about walking pace, I suppose. They were everywhere. They were all going about the grass, like when you want to herd a lot of sheep. They always do pick a wild night.

'Of course, I wish I'd had something there. I could have blocked it off and I would have done all right. But I had nothing with me and away they went off into the river and then out past Stert Island and God knows where they got to. And I've never seen the eels crossing over like that night since.'

One last note: it is difficult to kill an eel. You can stun them and then freeze them. You can freeze them alive. You can skin them alive by making a cut around the head and then rolling the skin off like a stocking down the body. Or you can salt them. They thrash in the salter for two hours until they dry out and die. Or, as they do in Germany, you can put them in a barrel full of washing powder which does the same thing. No way is exactly quick. There is a sobering and respectful superstition on the moors: do not eat an elver after Good Friday, as by then it can see. And remember: the eel will have lived for a while in the gut of a heron, in its most comfortable and close-fitting home of all.

If there is one harvest from the Levels more obvious than the eel, it is the peat itself. South of the Poldens, most of the moors are covered with an overburden of clay and almost no peat has been dug there. Further north, however, where drainage was always most difficult, and where between about 4,500 BC and AD 400 up to twenty feet of peat accumulated, hundreds of thousands of tons of Somerset have been dug up, put in plastic bags and pushed into endless gardens around the country to lighten the loam. Production is currently running at more than half a million tons a year.

As you cross the Poldens, leaving the intricate pattern of the Sedgemoor meadows and rhynes and come down towards the Brue, everything changes. The new country is a different colour. The green skin has been pared away and the blackness of the peat exposed. It is like a slate quarry gone soft. There is the atmosphere of necessary dereliction which surrounds any sort of quarrying but it is accompanied here by a sense of almost luscious waste, the smeared remains of a chocolate pudding with the spoon left half sunk in the cream. There is something primitive in the semi-derelict remains of the flooded peat pits, in the mineral oiled blackness of the water that fills them, in the rusted diesel pumps with elephant trunks dipped into the water, the comfrey sponging up around the machinery and the old brontosaur skeleton of a

On Godney Moor.

Walt Boucher cuts peat blocks on Ashcott Heath and George Rivet
watches: something primitive in the peat pits, like a slate quarry
gone soft.

digger or two with their tracks cast off and lying flat on the side. The Norfolk reed, *phragmites*, rushes and cotton-grass colonise the porridgy edges of the workings and after a while willow and alder sprout as a sort of scrubby fen woodland on the slightly higher patches. It is a beginning again, as though removing the peat had removed the whole history of accretion. If some disaster occurred, these plants would become the bottom layer reached by a new generation of peat extractors in six thousand years' time.

This almost tropical air of the two peat zones on either side of the Brue itself is heightened by the feeling of instant wealth, of a peat-rush bonanza that has gathered around it. It is a mixture unfamiliar in England, of new money on the very lip of old poverty, of the new landscape of wealth in pockets – ornamental pools – between the older broken structures of subsistence. Before the war, the wettest turf-ground could be had for £5 an acre. Now the same piece, unworked, still 'full-depth' and rechristened peat-land, is worth £10,000. The Levels are not conspicuous for their wealth but here you find golden Ferraris parked up gravel drives, sunbeds and bench-swings on geranium-fringed patios, a general riding-the-wave-of-success sensation, like a village in the jungle where every man has found oil in his back garden.

It is a landscape in the service of grow-bag tomatoes. The worked-out ground – or much of it – may be left to dereliction, but the still-valuable peat areas have an applied, business-like neatness about them. The German extraction machines – little self-sufficient factories on tank tracks, with springs, levers, fences, wires, cutters, a seat for the driver under a shade and an ejection chute, all of it making the movements of an animated puppet playing a concertina – deliver the sliced blocks at the side of the trench in neat little walls, patio parapets across the fields. The blocks are then piled in small airy beehives to dry before being taken to the corrugated processing sheds. There the peat stands in vast black-brown mounds sprouting weeds on one side, clawed at by grimy yellow diggers on the other.

Dried milled peat of the best quality can be worth £120 a ton. One of the digging machines can maintain an annual production from one acre of 100 tons. A man only needs fifty acres of this ground to get an annual turnover of £600,000. Over its lifetime, maybe sixteen years, an acre of peat will produce about 1,800 tons which after processing will be worth more than £200,000. Fifty acres of the very best peat land will produce £10 million worth of peat. This, of course, is not all profit – the plant and processing are expensive – but it gives some measure of the prize which farmers in the peat area have naturally turned to and which has transformed their lives.

Stan Durston is a peat man who lives in a smart villa on the edge of Meare. He has seen the whole cycle of change, from turf-cutter, one of the poorest people in the county, to peat-producer, one of the richest. 'I lived in Sharpham all my life until we moved up here. Snipe Farm. There was always the boat tied up at the back door. And I've seen it up the second step of the stairs in there. In the winter, Father used to take Mother in the boat with her bike. Then she used to cycle up to Street to get the groceries. Then he'd meet her again at the drove in the boat. There was no other way with the water being so high. You can imagine what it was like, us kids getting fed up with being housebound all winter.

'We didn't have any land out of the flood. But the peat fields themselves often didn't go underwater. It was the approaches that went under, where it had been taken away before. The droves, the tracks, were always under. They got dry and powdery in the summer and got blown away. You know what a blow is? They'd get powdery with the churning of the wheels and then in the winds, only a quarter or half an inch a year, the drove dropped down.

'We used to dig out the mumps, 28 lbs each, like fat blocks of black wet cheese they were, but heavy; it was heavy work. Put them on the flat barrow – it would be low so you didn't have to lift the mumps too far. Then they'd be cut in three, 10 by 8 by 1½, and you'd get twenty-five of them for 6d. Chuck 500 of them in the boat. Father knew where the water was deepest. He'd follow the ditches as a rule. The two feet of water on the land might not be enough for the boat. So then off the boat, on to the lorry,

An atmosphere of dereliction and waste inseparable from the
peatlands north of the Poldens.

Ducks, geese and abandoned fridges, Henley.

Walt Boucher cutting mumps on Ashcott Heath: the new life in the
flooded pit is a beginning again; these rushes will be the bottom layer
of the peat that will be cut in 6,000 years time.

Cottongrass on Birtle Heath flowering in the acid pools.

Wild iris and drying peat on Shapwick Heath: a near-tropical lushness.

John Vowles stacking machine-cut peat on Shapwick Heath: precise extraction of a valuable resource.

an old Model T Ford, left-hand drive, imported from the United States. There'd be two boat-loads to one lorry-load, a thousand blocks on the old tin lizzy. Then we'd drive them to a private house in Street. Father'd say: "Don't forget to touch your cap, she might give you a piece of cake." We'd wheel them in and stack them, and do you know how much we'd get for that lot – a thousand blocks, cut, dried, delivered, stacked? Twenty shillings, one pound sterling. They would have been drying since April. Two or three months to dry usually, first in the little hiles and then in the big ruckles. But you don't know how long it takes to dry. It all depends on Allah.

'We used to make some sort of a living, I suppose, but you ask me about the change. Well, I thought I'd arrived when I sent 100,000 blocks to Japan for distilling whisky – bagged, on lorries. I got £400 for that lot. I suppose it was sometime in the early sixties. And, of course, I thought: *Here we go.* That was for two years but it turned out the whisky wasn't any good, so they didn't want the peat. You could say the wheel came off. I did cows for a bit. Then I got this order for a thousand tons of garden peat from E. J. Godwin. And since then we've never looked back. I do 12,000 ton a year now to Godwins. I've got four Hymacs. I'm on to my fourth digging machine. It's the most advanced model around here – over £28,000, that one. I've got 155 acres of peat ground, only fifteen of them worked out. I could sell more if I wanted to but the taxman would give me a hammering. If I keep it steady, I've got enough for my two boys for the rest of their working life.'

Peat production is levelling off as the producers themselves realise the stupidity of destroying a limited resource too quickly and as the County Council steadfastly refuses to extend the Peat Area beyond the two zones set up in 1967. There is an all too visible horizon at which the peat will be exhausted. A 3,000-acre hole will occupy the middle of Somerset like the neglected core of some old, sweet-chewing molar, surrounded by a whole community reminiscing over a better time when there was work and money. Six or seven hundred jobs depend on the peat at the moment. The future is a rather gloomy vision, a dreadful metaphorical landscape of the quick buck and the spent reserve. Not that Life Before Garden Centres was anything idyllic in the Brue Basin. Cutting peat for fuel was grim work. The women's job was to stack the bricks in hiles. The particularly damp conditions of the turf-cutters' cottages meant that rheumatism, the ague, and neuralgia in various forms were rife at all times of year. In many of the houses here now, people still keep photographs – even the patronising postcards – of life as it used to be: the family of seven outside the colour-washed cottage, the water brimming up past the picket fence into the garden, the air of frank despondency in front of the camera.

Modern drainage improvements mean that the desperate wetness of before the war will never return, but once the peat has gone things will never be the same here. There are various plans in the air to prevent Westhay Moor and Meare Heath from becoming a lowland Blaenau Ffestiniog, suitable only as a background of facile dereliction against which to stand swimming suits and Ford Granadas. Many of the extractors are obliged to return the land to agriculture when they have reached the clay. This is feasible with continuous pumping but the low land – ten feet or more below its previous level – is subject to frosts and plants will not grow well down there. Others want to keep the pits wet for wildfowling. The Nature Conservancy Council see great potential for it as a nature reserve, where dragonflies and damselflies could flourish, where new low-level and very wet meadows could be created, where there would be a whole complex of reed swamps, fen woodland, open water and herb-rich areas, some of it inaccessible, some on show. Tourism and farming would take up some of the jobs now in peat but most of them would disappear. Those who are less concerned for the wildlife of wetlands have suggested that the worked out areas could be used as rubbish dumps which would be sown when full and returned to agriculture that way. Nothing is decided.

*

This squalid half-mineral, which dirties its extractors and leaves its bed degraded and confused, which produces golden Ferraris glittering by the farms like pendants from a wrestler's neck, brings one more general reward. The peat is acid and poor in oxygen. Organic material – wood, fibre, pollen – is preserved within it. This peculiar property has meant the survival of a unique archaeological record of life on the Levels from the fifth millennium B.C. until the lake villages were abandoned not long before the coming of the Romans. It is this preservation of material which usually rots away that makes the archaeology of the Levels so spectacular. There is none of the skeletal hardness of the remains usually picked up from drier digs, the bony fragments of life between which the soft disposable parts have to be reimagined.

In the Levels, it is those more transient parts themselves which are preserved, the more malleable materials which still bear the exact impressions made by people on them. The actual slicing of Stone Age adzes remains on the wood. A stone arrow head still bears the gum and nettle binding with which it was fixed to its shaft. The gnaw-marks made by beavers can still be seen on poles that were re-used by Bronze Age men in the foundation of a jetty on the edge of the bog. A two-tined pitchfork made of a fat, naturally branching hazel was found in Skinner's Wood on Shapwick Heath. Long pins made of yew twigs have been found. They may have decorated Neolithic noses. As well as wooden net-floats and a few canoes, archaeologists have discovered the crude battered head and hunched torso of a little hermaphrodite god-dolly, with flattened breasts and the thick stump of a penis. It was found beneath a slipway which radio-carbon dates have put at around 2,900 B.C. The painters of the boats that were tied up there had rubbed notches in the wood. There is an immediacy and domesticity in the survival of these things which stone or metal could never approach.

The objects are first discovered when a ditch is cleaned, a drain widened or when the peat-diggers themselves expose a piece of worked wood in the trenches. The archaeologists then move in. The overburden of peat is removed by machine down to a few inches above the remains. Spades then take it to the top of the prehistoric timbers, but spatulas, fingers and ice lolly sticks are the only tools used in the exposure of the wood itself. Even then, it must be constantly wetted if it is not to shrivel away into uninformative twigs.

Most of the large-scale structures to have been discovered are wooden trackways laid across the marsh, either from one bit of high ground to another or to give access to the bog itself. Many of the trackways, which form a continuous series from about 4,000 to about 700 B.C., were made quite casually by throwing down bundles of brushwood in a rough line across the marsh. (In an extraordinary example of Levels continuity, Bob Thorne can remember using exactly this technique to make paths to his shrimp nets in Bridgwater Bay. More recently he has made do with breeze blocks.) Others were more elaborate, made of hurdles laid end to end. The regular diameter of the hazel sticks and the little kink at the bottom of some of them, where the shoot had grown out of a previously cut stump, shows that Stone Age men in the Levels managed woodland by coppicing. It is the first known example of woodland management in Europe.

Outstanding among all the trackways is the earliest, the Sweet Track, which has been dated to about 3,800 B.C. It was discovered in 1970 when Ray Sweet, a peat-digger, saw an ashwood plank in the side of a ditch he was cleaning on Shapwick Heath. The trackway has now been traced for over a mile between a small sandy ridge, a burtle, just north of the Poldens and the island of Westhay/Meare. It is the most elaborate of all the trackways so far discovered, designed to provide a raised walkway above the wet surface of the bog. First, a pole was laid on the peat and fixed there with two long pegs driven across it at oblique angles. Peat was then piled on top of the pole to about ten inches or a foot above the surface of the bog. An oak plank, the narrow walkway itself, was laid on top of the low peat bank between the projecting tops of the oblique pegs. The plank was then

fixed to the rest of the structure with more pegs, three feet long, driven vertically down through the plank and into the underlying clay. Tall posts from a previous track along the route, which had proved unsatisfactory because it was not raised above the bog but laid on it, accompanied the Sweet Track for long stretches, possibly with a rope strung between them.

A brilliant analysis of the growth rings on the Sweet Track timbers has allowed archaeologists to identify the particular trees from which different planks were cut. By matching growth rings from different planks, they have found that timber from the same tree is distributed widely along the length of the track. It is certain that the wood was felled, split into planks and stockpiled off-site during the winter before being moved out on to the bog and used in the construction of the walkway. This speaks of a degree of organisation but the detective work has gone further. It turns out that different stretches of the track were built with timber from utterly different sorts of woodland. The oak in southern sections came from quick-growing, slender trees, the typical pattern of regrowth after clearance; that from northerly sites was from mature, ancient forest, slow-growing, with narrower rings. It is possible that the difference in the oak in different parts of the track actually records the expansion of the Neolithic economy in the Brue basin, as it moved out from the long-established fields and managed woods of the Poldens to the virgin territory of the Westhay island. There the forest was cleared to make way for new fields which the track itself gave access to.

It is this detailed quality in the archaeology of the Levels which makes it so exciting. The motives, the organisation, even the mental processes of the people who built the track are recoverable in the details of its remains. The way in which various pegs have been sharpened, some like a pencil, some like a chisel, may represent the different techniques of individual craftsmen. The presence of pollen in the peat from sorrels and docks and other grassland weeds like ribwort plantain, together with a significant drop in tree pollens around the time of the track, point to a large-scale clearance of woodland and its replacement with pasture for sheep and cows. A few grains of cereal pollen have also been found and of an arable weed – mugwort – which suggest a few wheat and barley fields too.

The picture accumulates. Under one part of the Sweet Track, the archaeologists found a small toy axe, made of two bits of oak. But a toy or a totem? That is where the evidence becomes inarticulate. The specifics are preserved but they are *frustratingly* specific. Two beautiful axe heads, one flint and one jadeite, were found embedded next to the track, both unused. There were some pots too, one full of cob nuts and another with a wooden stirrer. But there is something very odd about the pots. They were not the usual coarse domestic ware, but of the finest Neolithic workmanship, several of them coated in a black clay slip, burnished before firing and with a shiny black finish. Nobody knows why such luxury pots should be found here.

These are the oldest mysteries in a landscape full of them. To see the students on the dig, picking at the peat in the rain, as it turns from rust brown to black in its first air for six thousand years, is like watching a search for something lost, scrabbling after some fragmentary secret in the oldest residue of life on the Levels. The same constraints, give or take, applied then as do now: the winter floods, the high water table, the critical difference made by a rise of two or three feet in the level of the land. The Sweet Track was submerged each winter, when the men living on the islands cut timber to repair it as soon as the moor dried in the spring. (Archaeologists can tell the time at which timber is felled: if the last growth ring in

An archaeologist waters the timbers of the Stone Age Sweet Track, built in about 3,800 B.C., to prevent them drying out and disintegrating. This is the oldest made roadway in the world.

the wood is complete, the tree or branch was taken in the winter; if incomplete, in the spring or summer.)

The Sweet Track has one last surprise. It was in use for no more than ten years before the peat built up around the structure and engulfed it. Alder trees colonised the ridge and, as it would have remained slightly above the level of the surrounding bog, people would have continued to use it, for some years at least. It is a measure of the confidence of the Neolithic culture in the Levels that so much care and work was put into a structure whose builders must have known that it would last such a short time. It is not the work of people leading a marginal or desperate existence, but of a society absolutely in tune with the place it occupies. The Sweet Track is one of the great monuments to the life of human beings in the Somerset Levels – for its literal rising above difficulties, its inventiveness and intelligence, its refusal to be deterred by circumstances, its use of materials, its rational imposition of a sort of order on a wilderness, its evidence of cooperation between people. You could ask for nothing more.

Archaeologists can redeem fragments from a past which is otherwise obscure – the particular blows of a man making pegs, the flowering of mugwort in a field of emmer wheat, the preparation in winter of repair-wood for the coming spring – but for the quality of life in the Levels, for the way in which people lived, one must wait. Jump to the seventeenth century and another side becomes clear. Illness was chronic. Malnutrition led to eye complaints, eruptions on the skin, scurvy and rickets. Bad food and contaminated water made things worse. Tuberculosis was rampant among teenagers. There was rheumatism and arthritis in all ages of the population. Taunton had a smallpox epidemic every seven years

throughout the century and life expectancy hovered somewhere in the mid-thirties. About one in five infants died and, of every ten babies born, four died before they were fifteen. One girl in three survived to have children herself. Four-fifths of the income of the very poor went on food, of which the most expensive item was bread. One in every four or five harvests was bad and a poor harvest catapulted such families into starvation.

In years of dearth, it would not be the winter itself but the following springtime, as the Levels began to flower and the food ran out, in which people would suffer. Rather than starve, they would turn to crime. Prosecutions for theft jumped 250% in bad years and in the Levels show a fascinating annual pattern which does not occur in other parts of the county. In the winter, with the floods, the number of prosecutions drops away, to rise again with the drying in the springtime. One is left with the picture of seasonal freedoms, of a communal delight at the coming of the protective floods, when all the usual restrictions and impositions were suspended and the traditional role of the wetness of the moors – isolating communities in a temporary freedom from authority – could be found again.

A system of mutual fostering operated in which children went to live with the neighbours as their servants and where discipline was brutal and frequent. This terrible childhood of most peasants, separated from their families when they were four or five and cruelly treated by their new masters, produced in its turn cruel, cold and suspicious adults, liable to outbursts of hostility and extraordinary violence. On the undrained moors, some of the poorest land in the country, the pressures of poverty must have made this life a hell. One buffer existed against complete dissolution: the common rights to cut turf, collect rushes and sedge, to 'shroud' or pollard the trees, to take fish and fowl and to pasture animals on the

Excavating the Sweet Track: scraping away with spatulas, ice-lolly sticks and fingernails.

Dr Michael Richards holds a surgery in the parlour of the King's Head, High Ham. Tuberculosis, rheumatism and the all-purpose ague were endemic among the population of the Levels until this century.

Bridgwater Horse Fair: the best Levels horses had enormous feet to spread the weight and stop them sinking into the moorland fields.

*George 'Ginger' David of Burrow Bridge milking one of his thirteen
cows.*

moors. The undrained land represented a common reservoir on which even the poorest could draw. It is this background which must be understood in the repeated stories of peasant resistance to grand drainage schemes. If a moor was drained and divided up, the common rights held by all the people disappeared.

The classic instance in the seventeenth century was King's Sedgemoor, entirely owned, as its name implies, by the crown. The Stuart monarchy was desperate for money and the draining of the moor represented a handsome opportunity. Agents were appointed, plans drawn up and negotiations opened with the freeholders who had rights of common on the moor. The Agents reported that 'the very ditches of the enclosures will so drayne it, sucke out the water and the land will soon become warm, solide and full of fruite.' This may have been optimistic but it was not on technical grounds that the scheme failed.

The prospect of the extinction of their common rights made the freeholders resist. Their obstinacy, their defence of independence and their simple obstructionism made any progress impossible. Eventually, in 1632, Charles I sold off 4,000 acres of the unimproved moor at £3 an acre. The main agent, John Battalion, was summoned before the Attorney General in 1635 to explain the failure. In words which exactly reflect the intransigent siltiness of the moors and the moor-men, he explained how the whole business 'had fylled and cloyed with many more perplexityes, questions and queres than I ever dreamt.' That is the reality of the place, of its natural conservatism and refusal to be cowed by higher authority. When, in the eighteenth century, the more elaborate scheme for the moor was introduced, it met with the same sort of opposition, which this time failed. As one enthusiastic improver complained: there is no propriety in 'calling a publick meeting with a view of gaining signatures of consent. . . . At all publick meetings of this nature that I ever attended noise and clamour have silenced sound sense and argument. Once men have joined the opposition, their pride will not let them relent.'

Harold Hembrow has his ancestors. Cutting the bank was not invented by his father or Uncle Sam Winchester. There is an almost continuous record of prosecutions against bank-cutters from the thirteenth century to the twentieth. It represents an independence which emerged in their flocking to the nonconformist chapels (although John Wesley never found a more boorish congregation than the one at Fivehead), perhaps in their support for Monmouth and certainly in their resistance in more recent years to the interference of conservation bodies with their own rights on their own land.

This cord of self-reliance which runs through the heart of the Levels – it is tangible enough but difficult to describe – may have been the product originally of terrible poverty and hardship (a traveller through Somerset in 1880 found a whole family in Athelney chewing quids of tobacco, passed down from father to wife to children, to stave off the hunger) – but it has grown well beyond that, so that for Harold Hembrow, who has lived all his life off piecework, never chained to one farmer or his whims, there is a pride and humour in the rascal independence of his life. He is no man's man but his own. The hardness of the life need not be underestimated. His back is long gone from years of bending to cut the withies. Leonard Meade's knees are wrecked from kneeling to make baskets for forty years. Bad backs and spoilt joints are endemic among the men of the moors, but the hardship has not been deadening. It has been a spur to resilience in these people, who are as shrewd as any, the best gossips in England and generous at any time.

The remains of a barter system survives in places: in the large vegetable gardens lined up along the Parrett from Stathe to Burrow Bridge, as trim as samplers in their ranks of vegetables and roses. There is always too much for the man or family living there, but the garden will provide a lettuce for someone dropping in, a cabbage as part payment for the milk, a bag or two of beans for a bottle or two of Guinness in the King Alfred or at Eli's up at Huish. When the Stuckeys managed to catch thirty hundredweight of carp one day in the lock below

Mervyn Fear's garden on Godney Moor: a tradition of growing enough vegetables to give some away.

Ena Hembrow's roadside stall at Burrow Bridge.

Dennis Wright stooking long-stemmed Maris Huntsman wheat
for thatching.

John Hector in the Burrow Bridge bakery.

East Brent Harvest Home used to be a series of drunken celebrations given by the farmers to their workers and friends at the end of the harvest. The tradition has now been replaced by a single festival for the whole village. It is no coincidence that the puddings, for which there is a prize, are exactly the shape of the Knoll which overlooks the village and after which the pub is named.

John Uppham of Stoke St Gregory cutting Fred Cousins's hair.

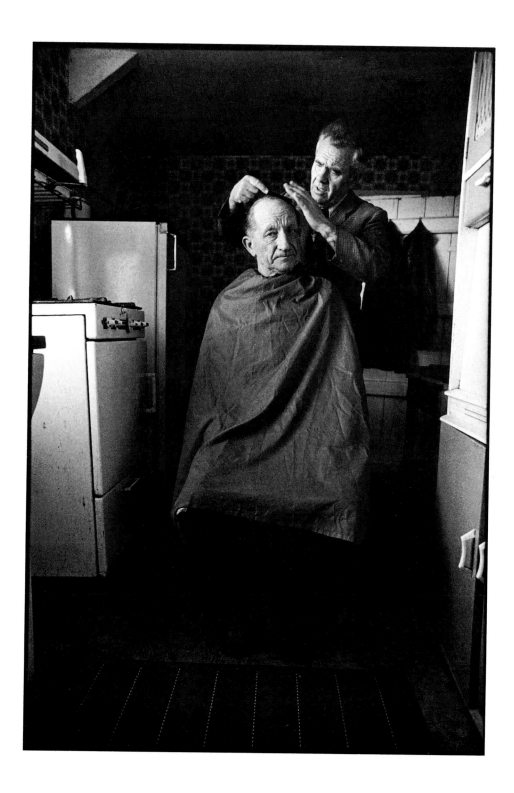

Langport they quite naturally distributed them among the poor of the town. (Its economy had collapsed with the decline in river traffic.) Arthur Stuckey can remember how 'the old farmer out the back here always put in a half acre of turnips and a half acre of swedes for the poor of Langport to go out and help theirselves. And if you'd done any jobs for him, like in haymaking, you'd get a lump of beef, twenty or thirty pounds. He used to fat his bullocks, then Christmas he would have a couple killed and distribute them out to the people who had helped. That was Frank Griffith. It was worse then, if you would, but twas better.'

This is the real fabric, the weave of the place, where people have survived in some of the most naturally atrocious conditions in the country and where like the builders of the Sweet Track, they have erected something definite above it – not grand, but reliable, well-made, useful, to be valued, civilised. As Harold says: 'It's been a hard life, but it's been a good life.'

And of course there has always been the cider. Not being an arable country, corn was always at a premium here. Brewing beer may have meant going without bread. Apple trees could be grown on the moors themselves but the peat made the apples – and the cider – black and unpalatable. This left the high ground and, at least until the war, orchards used to line the roads that ran along the islands and ridges above the Levels. The demand for cider was enormous. Every man, woman and child in seventeenth-century Somerset drank the equivalent of a quart of cider a day and, until the end of the nineteenth century, wages were made up with an allowance of cider, maybe three pints daily in the winter, rising to a gallon or more at the hay cut. This notorious system – the cider truck – at least meant payment was on time. When it was replaced by money, the labourer was often forced to wait until the farmer had sold the goods he had produced – the withies or the hay – before he received the benefit. In a world of piecework, there was no redress and if things turned bad they entered a vicious cycle. Less money meant less food meant you could do less work and earn less money.

In living memory, the consumption of cider was prodigious. Harold Hembrow as a child used to drink a pint of cider before going to school every day. Later, when cutting hay or withies, he often drank a gallon or even two in the day's work. The firkin used to be hung in a rhyne to cool, pegged to the bank with a string and a stick.

Various questions arise: why, even outside the hot hay time, were these people so thirsty? And how, with this amount of cider inside you, could you work at all? Until the nineteenth century, it was the only drink for the Levels' poor. Tea, coffee and chocolate were aristocratic pleasures. Milk was thought fit only for children. River water was pretty bad, well water nasty. Cider was simply the best fluid available. The dull and repetitive cereal diet made you listless and gave you a craving for stimulants. If bread, porridge and pulses had some relief on the menu, it was likely to be in the form of salty meat or salty fish, which would only increase the thirst.

Cider also makes you drunk. Keith Thomas has described it as 'an essential narcotic against the pettiness, fear and maliciousness of contemporary parish life'. Drink at least pads poverty. Harold Hembrow defines 'cidered up' as 'still drinking but on the floor when you're doing it'. He can no longer take any cider himself. The acid in it has done terrible things to his gut. (If you put a slab of steak in a barrel of cider, feeding it, as they say, the meat will disappear within a few days, eaten by the acid, and the drink will have acquired a ghostly new thickness, the *body* of dissolved beef.)

But how could one work on the quantities of cider that were said to be drunk? Some people maintain that only when halfway to being cidered up, could you really get into the swing of the scythe.

Harold: 'In they days, it used to be different to what it is now. You would get your lotion of cider before you started. Load up the old wagon. Cidered up. I think I've drunk more cider than I have anything else. Everything used to get done by hand, but it used to get done. There

In the White Hart, North Curry. It is said that the best cider always looks milky.

Clifford Crossman, a cider maker at High Ham. The only possible
word for being drunk on cider is 'hammered'.

was nothing else for it. Haymaking from five or six in the morning till eleven, till twelve at night. Pick it about, get it dry, load it, unload it and perhaps get back there again. They never used to bother about going to bed. You see, Adam, I can't make out now how we used to stick it. The bread and cheese and pickled onion would keep ee going. The *cider* would keep ee going.'

Even so, there is another point. The cider that would be given to the labourers would be the 'second wringing', after the farmer's 'own drinking' had already been taken from the press. To every hogshead of this second wringing, four gallons of hopwater were added to keep it from turning to vinegar. This second tap, if ever sold, was worth no more than a third or a half of the farmer's own drinking. A gallon or two of this would not, if you had been drinking it virtually since birth, have been a great intoxicant.

Stan Hall, a cider maker at Fordgate near Moorland, who now calls his own product HTV Cider because it has appeared in so many television documentaries, puts it down to a change in the quality of men. 'In the old-fashioned days, you give a boy a gallon of cider and he goes out to work with his farmhouse cheese and farmhouse butter and what you'd call a granary loaf, I suppose. That'd be all right, he'd sweat that out. Now you give a bloke a gallon of cider today, he's pissed as a newt. They're all dole-wallopers, the lot of them.'

Rather confusingly, Harold maintains that the labourers' cider was the best. 'It would be stronger than it is now. The second pressing was the best, strongest, wasn't it? The last pressing was always the strongest because we always reckoned when we go to the last pressing, that's when you squeeze the pips out and that's when the best of the cider was made. When you come to the third pressing, you take it all out and crumble it up and put it all back up again for the last gallon, because that was the strongest. When you press it down and it was that tight, and you could see the pips flying out, that was when the best of the cider was coming out.'

There was one great exception to the universal consumption of cider. Chapel men might refuse to drink it at all. This was seen as the most self-regarding affectation by non-sectarians who had a defensive jeer of their own about it: a man going to church might carry a bible in one hand and a pint of cider in the other but a Baptist going to his devotions always had the good book in one hand and his prick in the other.

Nothing could be further from the sour draught of the second tap than the look of the orchards themselves. They are not continuous along the roadside as they used to be. The acreage of orchards in the Levels dropped from nearly 4,500 in 1966 to a little over a third of that figure at the end of the seventies. Each orchard that now survives is a patch cut from a long green tapestry. Sit there on a June morning. The blossom floats down in a snowstorm as notional as in one of those glass-bubble scenes of winter in Lapland. The trunks have leant like gravestones over the years and heifers grazing under them scratch a flank on the bark. Old apple trees die from the feet up. The dead branches hang out at the bottom, as if the trees had had a sort of communal stroke. Each continues to live only in its upper half, its arms and head, leaving the older limbs juiceless and decayed. There is no mistletoe on the dead timber but, higher up, bundles of the odd green rubbery plant erupt through the apple bark like a submarine parasite in the branches of a coral.

Under them all, in this room of trees, there is an indescribable sweetness in the light, a dew-rimmed cool. This limpid clarity somehow produces a drink of which the test of excellence is the viciousness with which it cuts your throat from the inside and the violence with which it pulps the back of your skull. No drunkenness is better described as 'being hammered'. It is not a particularly happy one but forgetful, a sort of dazed floating, neither high nor low, in which life is planed down to its easiest simplicities and then comfortably suspended from springs.

There will be a corrugated shed near the orchard. In the summer, it is a dry, musty place with the memory of old

Tom Hodge and Joan Norris gathering Morgan Sweet cider apples
in their orchard at Henley on the edge of King's Sedgemoor.

A mound of apples awaiting pressing at Helland on the edge of West Sedgemoor. The best cider, it is said, is made from good apples and a little rot.

Lewis Boobyer and his sons building a cider cheese with straw and
pomace — the pulp of apples crushed in the mill on the right — in
Kenny Pimms's cider house at Burrow Bridge.

Don Coate pressing a cheese at Helland. Juice runs from the straw like sweat.

pressings in the air. The air is stained with the memory of cider like an odd lost warmth. Here in autumn the cider is made. It will always be late on, the later the better as a little bit of rot adds flavour to the drink and makes it clearer in the glass. The trees will have been shaken, and a good mixture of sweet, sharp and acid apples gathered in supermarket trolleys and old feed bags. First, they are milled into a pomace which is then laid on the bed of the press, lined with fresh straw. Fusty straw will eventually clog the palate. Oak or aluminium shovels must be used. Steel corrodes in the acid. Alternate layers of straw and pomace are piled on the bed of the press to build the 'cheese'. The straw filters the apple juice and gives the pomace, a pulp, enough structure to withstand the pressure. The 'follower' is lowered towards the bed and juice runs from the cheese like a night sweat. The press is tightened with an enormous spanner and the little sill of the bed brims with the sweet fresh syrup and runs curving like the Tone from the spout into the waiting tub. Children hold cups next to the leaking straw to catch the juice. The men drink last year's cider. If the juice is sticky on the arms, the sugar is high and the cider will be good.

From the tub by the spout of the bed, the cider goes into the vats. Oak is best, chestnut cheaper and 300-gallon black plastic Israeli fruit juice containers the usual alternative. The purists object. Julian Temperley – who makes cider near Kingsbury Episcopi, wins prizes and supplies both the Glastonbury Festival and the re-enactments of the Battle of Sedgemoor on Westonzoyland aerodrome – mixes a sympathy for the Palestinians with an enthusiasm for older techniques. 'Israel is where the plastic things come from and Israel is where they deserve to stay. In an oak vat, the tannins of the wood go back into the cider. It matures. It can't mature in Israeli plastic. They're a horrible cheapskate answer. They'll be the death of cider. If you haven't got barrels, you shouldn't be able to call it cider.' This is the extreme position of a man who sees, justifiably enough, the future of real cider under threat.

The extraordinary success of 'Taunton Cider', to use a generic term ('They've got a man in a white coat, and an assistant in a white coat and when it comes to mucking around, they make a job of it, and produce a good industrial cider, *jolly* good, quite weak, same colour year in, year out – it's a normal industrial product: 10% water') – the extraordinary success of this has put the small cider-makers under pressure. Many of them, instead of trying to improve their own kind of drink, have tried to compete with the big cider factories, committing Temperley's cardinal sin of *adding*: saccharine, colouring, the by-products of ICI, making it out of concentrate, even *grape* concentrate. These are temptations which never had to be resisted in the past. It was always the most local of products in which the only materials to hand were the apples. A clouded, cloggy, yeast-thick, dull-looking vinegar tasting of old socks could be the elixir itself in one village and enough to make the pigs sick over the hill. Harold Hembrow, to take a random example, used to be a great addict of Harold Meade's cider in Athelney. It came in three varieties: sweet (lots of honey and brown sugar), shit-shirt and binding. A pint of shit-shirt had to be quickly followed with a pint of binding if disaster was not to strike. All three were cloudy and Harold Hembrow insists that cider *should* be cloudy. In Kingsbury, no more than seven miles away, a pint of very cloudy cider could not find a buyer.

This local quality of cider is precious. It is – or now perhaps, was – the lubricant of tight communities. Cider played its role in the system of good for good, service for service. It may have been a necessary narcotic but it was also part of a system in which there was a short and obvious journey between production and consumption, between the life of people on the Levels and the materials and tools with which they made that life work. The system survives in pieces, but that description may be a contradiction in terms. The virtue of it – and one condition of its existence may have been poverty – was the inter-reliance of the physics, the biology and psychology of the place. It was the links that

Phyllis Champion in the Burrow Bridge Post Office.

At the Wedmore Harvest Home.

Charlie Showers singing the wassail in Drayton to usher out the old year and welcome in the new.

On Common Moor below Glastonbury.

Ruth Colbeck and the children at Meare village school.

In Westhay.

mattered, that made the extraordinary wholesomeness of the Levels and created its dominant air of congruity, of being fitted to itself. Such a thing cannot survive in pieces. If the links are broken, there is a dispersal of energies, an interruption in the flow of place back into place, in the self-confirming network of thought, intention, work, reward and investment. This breakdown is both a release and a deprivation. The bonds of small rural societies both constrain and support, both enable and disable, and their ending is both good and bad.

There is no doubt that it has happened here. Change has come to the Levels. It has come late because it was a poor place and poverty is conservative. Even now, it is visibly in transition and, paradoxically enough, full of *incongruities* and of abrupt transitions: of real herons standing next to their neater plastic brothers on a pondside, of the Italian-moccasined sons of fathers who have straw in their hair, of tourist enterprise burgeoning in industries such as the withy-growing a mile away from other men in the same business who are gripped in the last whimpering phases of decline.

Dick House, the farmer from Stoke St Gregory, told me that before the war things were just like the good life. This seemed to be conventional enough as a form of nostalgia until he said: 'I've always liked Felicity Kendal.' He was talking about a television programme on suburban vegetarians; not the good life but *The Good Life*. 'It was hell on earth,' he said. 'We didn't live in the proper sense of the word some years. We just didn't die.' The Levels are now in the middle of a massive, rolling transformation. You see it everywhere but can never quite grasp it. As Arthur Stuckey says: 'Things keep changing. You just can't remember when they do, can you?'

The withies that are grown to make baskets provide a history of at least one sort of change. They have been found binding Neolithic hurdles laid on Walton Heath and a carbonised base of a willow basket was found in the Iron Age lake village near Glastonbury. These withies were probably clipped from a naturally growing willow tree and tied in there green. The willow is a pioneer, creeping up over the damp earth as the ice-sheets drew back, and its natural resilience, its ready shooting after being shorn to a stump, has always made it useful. The salicylic acid in the bark has long been used as a drug against fevers. It is the basis of aspirin. The leaves and bark can be used in tanning leather. The wood is strong for its weight, good for clogs and artificial limbs. The twisted bark of very young shoots can be used as string. Keepers of vineyards habitually planted one acre of willows for every twenty-five of grapes to provide the string and poles on which to train the vines.

Levels men have always cut the willows that grow naturally. Bob Thorne takes them out of the hedge for his salmon butts fixed to the bed of the Parrett estuary at Black Rock. He uses two-year sticks for the structure and one-year withies to bind them. 'The river runs so hard that wire wouldn't stick it. It would buckle. Withy is like a spring. It will vibrate where metal won't. You get out there when the butts is just opening at a spring and it's two foot six higher at the mouth than at the tail. There's *tons* of pressure there and metal wouldn't take it. Withy's the only stuff that will.' Leonard Meade, the basket-maker from Burrow Bridge, still makes an occasional eel trap from green withies, but the demand is now from museums and collectors who will never use them. The traps lasted one season if they were used in a rhyne but will remain for ever, drying, if posed in a folk-life display.

Something of the ancient style of cropping from the natural willow is still to be seen in the pollarded trees that fringe the ditches and rhynes. They are there partly to strengthen the banks, partly to mark the droves in the floods and partly as a renewable resource, lifted above the grazing mouths of the cattle. The sticks are cut in the winter every three years or so and used for chair legs, the stakes in larger baskets, as thatching spars to peg the wheat reed into the roof, or simply for burning. Nothing looks worse than a recently pollarded willow – the local word is shrouded – but in the springtime, new sprigs burst out all over the head of the shorn stump and by

New Road Farm in East Huntspill.

Joan and Florence Tucker, farmers on Tealham Moor.

98

Withies on West Sedgemoor.

Stan Derham pollarding a willow, a form of tree-management that has been used on the Levels since the Bronze Age. It guarantees a regular crop of sticks for furniture and firewood.

Harold Wright, the thatcher, splits willow sticks to make pegs or 'spars' that hold the thatch in place.

midsummer the shrouded willows appear as green-topped button mushrooms along the ditches. Even if lightning has split and charred the cabled, knitted trunk, gutting it, fresh life will stand out at the head. In fact, if the pollard is to survive at all, the branches must be cut at regular intervals. If they are allowed to grow too tall and heavy the short trunk cannot take the weight and the tree will split or keel over and die.

Until the beginning of the nineteenth century, this foraging for willow wood and withies in the naturally occurring bushes and trees was sufficient. Not until some time after 1810 was the first withy bed planted on West Sedgemoor. It is one of the easiest crops to sow. Short lengths of willow sticks called sets are simply pushed into the ground, about 19,000 to an acre, and they start growing there. (Willow sticks that are used to mark rows of vegetables, for example, will take root and become trees. A willow fence will become a willow hedge with no encouragement.) Farmers looked on the crop as a novelty at first but, with the Victorian fad for wicker furniture, the withy business took off. Mr Slocombe in North Petherton began the manufacture of the diamond-back chairs for which Somerset became famous. Few examples now survive but they are pretty and delicate with an open lattice of one-year-old withies across the back. The making of baskets on a commercial scale grew out of the furniture business but, before the First World War, fashions changed, wicker furniture lost its appeal and of necessity baskets became the staple of the growers. Virtually the whole economy of North Curry, Stoke St Gregory, Burrow Bridge and Stathe depended on the withies in the 1920s. About a thousand acres were devoted to the withy beds on the surrounding moors, with another five hundred south of Langport.

When the slump came it was ruinous. A bundle of withies was worth 27/- in the early 1920s. By 1935 the price had crashed to 4/6. Many of the smaller men simply went out of business and the acreage under willow shrank by two-thirds. Baskets, which had been the essential containers for any number of industrial and agricultural purposes, began to be replaced by modern materials.

Withy-growing and basket-making are extraordinarily labour-intensive and it is an industry with more processes than most: folding animals in the beds early in the spring to hold the withies back until after the frosts; two or even three weedings of the beds a year by hook or hoe; a spray or two with a nicotine solution; cutting the withies by hand, a long and back-breaking job both in the bending and the carrying, which could only be done in the winter after the fall of the leaf; trimming the stocks if the cutting had been fast or the cutter inexperienced and if the next year's withy was not to have a useless heel at the base; bundling the cut withies; transporting them from the bed to the yard, the first part by hand as no cart could come out on to the moor where the cutters, in the days before gumboots, were up to their shins in water, the source of endless agues and cramps; sorting the withies into sizes by heights; boiling those which were to be buffs for eight hours in a coal-fired boiler which had to be loaded, stoked and unloaded by hand and in which the water, a mineralised slick, stiff with tannin, had to be changed after every seven loads; 'steaming' those which were to be browns in the same water, but for a shorter time; keeping the best withies back for 'whites' in specially prepared ditches or pits from which the mud – or most of it – had to be cleaned out each year if the whites were not to be stained (Kenny Pimms of Burrow Bridge can remember picking a bundle of whites out of his ditch to find them solid with the eels that had crept in there); and then the stripping of the willows which, almost until the war, was done by hand, the work of women and children, in pairs of metal prongs called brakes through which each withy had to be drawn individually to peel off the skin. With the buff, it is relatively easy: the boiling turns the young bark into a sloppy orange skin that can be run off with a thumbnail to reveal the smooth dampness of the core underneath. Stripping the more valuable whites is a slower and more difficult job which can be done only for a short period in the spring as the sap is rising in the ditch-stored wads and before they begin to grow a second skin. Only the browns go unstripped.

A newly pollarded willow on King's Sedgemoor. In the spring new shoots will appear all over the head of the shorn stump.

A machine to do the job was invented in the thirties in which a handful of withies could be stripped at one time by pushing them across a revolving drum lined with miniature brakes. This may be quicker but it is more exhausting as the revolving pegs catch at the withies and pull the operator in towards the machine. For the long hours of a working day, he must haul back against it, twisting the withies around as he does so, shutting his ears to the roaring rattle of the machine and his nostrils to the acrid smell of bruised willow. The stripped buffs must then be tied up again in bundles for selling. All this has to be done before a single square inch of basket is made.

In the making of a basket, the intensity of labour is concentrated still more. All the strength of a basket represents work. The material itself has no strength in it and all the tension in a basket, the tightness in the weave, has been put in there by the maker. You only have to watch a man at work, with the long stakes rattling like the feathers of a peacock tail, to understand that a basket preserves not only the skill of a craftsman but a great deal of his energy. There is a resistance in the willow and the basket-maker has constantly to overcome its tendency to spring back out against the constraints of structure, constantly shifting the half-made object on his knees, struggling with the reluctance of the willow to take the required shape, a reluctance which will eventually give the basket its strength. Once you have realised this, every basket takes on a new character, as the diary of one man's morning.

It is also the product of a series of extraordinarily complicated movements which no one has yet succeeded in mechanising. They become embedded in the mind of the maker, a repeated pattern which requires effort but little vigilance. As Leonard Meade explains: 'For years, you've been going to sit down in a particular place. If you move that chair, you find yourself sitting on the floor, don't you? Well, you make a basket in the same way.'

It is not surprising that with this suite of complex, time-consuming skills, basketware could put up no resistance to plastics and injection moulding. The days when the seats of Sopwith Camels were made out of wicker might as well be in the Bronze Age.

You can still find abandoned withy beds on West Moor near Thorney and on West Sedgemoor itself. They are mysterious places. The withies have branched long ago into low bushy trees. Bindweed – called withy-wind here – brambles, nettles and vetch clog the miniature forest. It is a damp, equatorial and rather sinister place. Animals have beaten out twisting paths between the stocks. It is, like the peat-working, a form of reversion, of remembering. Control and vigilance have been removed, the great human brake on the life of the Levels has been allowed to relax and nature has accelerated into the vacuum. It is as though there is an equation here, with human work on one side and the expansions of nature on the other. Reduce one, abandon one, and the other will benefit.

Withies surged during the war, when one or two fortunes were made, as baskets were found to be the most shockproof of containers, ideally suited for anything to be dropped by parachute. In the wartime timber shortage, one man was buried in a basketware coffin. But after the war, the decline resumed its course. Foreign withy growers – especially in Belgium – began to export their willows to Britain. Cheap baskets from all over the world began to colonise large parts of a shrinking market.

There was a time when one of the large-scale growers in Curload near Athelney could buy a new Jaguar every year on the back of the withies, but not today. George Bawden, a small operator in Burrow Bridge, is now struggling with withy beds well past their best days and

Charlie Langford cutting withies: 'A peculiar deftness . . . no swipe but a quick, slight movement, either from the shoulder or the wrist.'

George Bawden, withy grower and boiler of Burrow Bridge. 'It isn't all honey.'

Ray Beck stripping buffs in one of the sheds belonging to the Coates at Meare Green: 'For the long hours of a working day the operator must haul back against the machine, twisting the withies around as he does so, shutting his ears to the rattle and his nostrils to the acrid smell of bruised willow.'

Emrys Coate sorting willows in Meare Green.

Alf Brewer and audience. Every basket is the diary of one man's morning.

Stan Dare making hurdles in Curload, weaving the spraggly sticks,
which are useless for baskets, between the thicker upright sails.

which now appear to be highly vulnerable to disease. Too high a proportion of his withies now fail to come up to the basket-makers' standards and have to go into hurdles. A large stack of them in his yard under the canopy of some old leaning apple trees are both too 'spraggly' for the basket-makers and too short for hurdles. They will probably be burnt. Others had been inexplicably stunted, probably by some herbicide drifting over from a nearby field. His coal-fired boiler had expanded with the heat and split its brick cladding. This was only to be expected but the split had run deep and the cladding probably needed more than the usual repair of river mud pushed into the crack. The withy business down here was not, as both Bawden and his split boiler said quite frankly, 'all honey'. He expects it to fizzle out in a year or two.

No more than a mile or two up the road, the prospects are very different. The Coates, whose son Jonathan is the champion rayballer, are the kings of the withy business. They have the most mechanised system of managing the bundles that come in from the beds and the most advanced marketing techniques in Somerset. Even so, the market is not the only vagary with which willow-growers have to deal. Their lives are dominated by disease and weather.

Chris Coate: We've been spraying for aphids all right. We'll call anything an aphid that's a bother. We've been plagued with elephants. That's a little beetle with a trunk on. Then there's buttontop. That's a little caterpillar which makes the withy branch out. But we're not plagued with that too badly, the odd one or two. They get it more around Kingsbury. No, rust is our biggest problem. You must have seen the heap of cankered withies up there. You've got to pick them out. You can't send them on.

Anne: We saw it in the withy beds when they were eight inches high last year. A very bright rust patch at the bottom of the leaf, just down the bit of stem there.

Chris: It's spores on the ground. They burst and you get done.

Anne: It's a sensitive plant because it grows so fast. It doesn't take much to stop the top from growing and then you get the side shoots. And then it's no good for baskets

Chris: Then we got caught by a late frost. We let four acres go early – we let the cattle out early – and of course away they went. They were about a foot high when we had the frost. It was too late to do anything about it. We couldn't cut them and start again. It'll all go for hurdles.

Anne: It can be very depressing. You can get a bad summer and you get very . . . It *is* on a knife edge a lot of the time. You're dependent on it. You've got all your eggs in one basket, haven't you? (She laughs.)

Chris: We're very dependent on the weather. In the morning, other people look at the forecast at breakfast time and decide whether to take their umbrellas or they don't. But to us . . . it can be whether our crop is a failure or not.

Anne: Look at that frost.

Chris: This season has been very difficult. It's been so cold, they've been stuck at six inches for weeks. It's not like it is for the farmers. The odd field of hay which you spoil with the wet weather, it's not everything. But when it's everything that you're doing, it's more of a . . . it *is* a worry. A dry summer doesn't worry them. What they like is warmth. They can take the water out of the ground. Even in '76, they were a good length. They weren't all fives. No, what they hate is spring floods. Water chills the ground and slows it up. It doesn't kill it. Nothing will kill a willow. You just don't get the height with the cold.

They have tried to broaden their base. Following the example of the Male family at Fivehead, the Coates have tried to grow teasels which are used to finish billiard cloths. But everything has its parasite. Eel-worms have eaten the seed in the ground and nothing has sprouted. They make willow into artist's charcoal in special ovens they had designed themselves but a neighbouring willow man has copied the ovens without permission and is planning to move into the market which the Coates pioneered. There will be a damaging trade war between them. The neighbour has also – to general consternation – imported a family of Corsican basket-makers who are

Anne Coate loading a box of willow sticks into an oven where they will be turned into artist's charcoal.

Alf Male carries teasels bound to a pole from his field at Fivehead. The teasels are used to raise the nap in the finishing of the finest cloths.

Charlie Langford on West Sedgemoor. 'The best cutter there was . . . the neatest man in Somerset.'

Malcolm Musgrave stacking willows after they have dried in the Coates' yard at Meare Green.

more adept at copying fashionable designs than the local men and women, who like Leonard Meade make willy butts and thirty-pound pickers in the same way that they sit in chairs.

These are the pressures of change but they are nothing new. The withy business was originally the child of fashion and the servant of industry. It now survives in the equally capricious market of the tourist trade and the nostalgia boom while still trying to portray itself, in Anne Coate's words, as 'the survival of a craft that goes back to King Alfred's day' Other problems are nearer at hand. It is difficult to find young men who will, or even can, cut the withies by hand.

Chris: Not everybody's trainable, are they? There are very few young cutters around. It will probably all be by machine in a few years. But the machine leaves the stump very untidy. And if you want to use a machine, you've got to start off with it. You couldn't put a machine into an old withy bed. The stump would be so big and you wouldn't know where you were cutting. Then you have to strim it afterwards. We *had* to use a machine last year. We would never have got through otherwise. We were a bit short of cutters. Poor old Charlie Langford died. He made a lot of difference. I know he went down and only cut twenty bundles a day (Harold Hembrow: What do you get paid a bundle nowadays? You get a bottle of Guinness a bundle, don't you?) but you do twenty bundles over three or four months and that adds up to a few acres. And Charlie was the best cutter there was. He was the neatest man in Somerset. His dying was only one part of a bad winter. It was a wet November and for a month after Christmas we couldn't cut a bundle. With that and Charlie dying, we *had* to use the machine. And that's the future, I suppose!

*

Harold Hembrow making a child's rattle from newly cut lengths of withy. Many of the more delicate basketry skills are now disappearing.

Like thatch, baskets are now luxury articles and if people still want to buy them, they will always be hand-made. But the peculiar deftness with which the cutters flick their hooks at the base of the long, blowing withies ('I've never seen them so measly thin! The whole lot are like bloody knitting needles.') – it is no swipe but a quick, slight movement, either from the shoulder or the wrist – will go. And with it, the bond of green withy to tie them up, the cold tea in the whisky bottle, the pinches of mentholated snuff, the sheltering from hailstones behind a windbreak made of cut withies leaning together – to be replaced by another set of particulars over which another generation will erect its own forms of nostalgia.

Basketry is no longer cheap and utilitarian. It has become something special, of which the main selling point is its *tone*, its association with some notional pre-industrial world. All this, in a way, models the recent history of the Levels themselves. Sedgemoor or Brent Marsh has always been a neglected, even a despised landscape. There is one extraordinary record of the first conservationist to have made his appreciation of the Levels known as early as 1816. Mr Parry, the manorial lord of Curry Rivel, very nearly blocked the first scheme to drain West Sedgemoor because it would have spoilt the lovely view of wilderness from his house.

But he was a rare spirit and other attitudes were more dismissive: 'This country has heretofore been much neglected, being destitute of gentlemen's houses, probably on account of the stagnant waters and unwholesome air . . .' (end of the eighteenth century); 'Either a gloomy waste of waters, or still more hideous expanse of reeds and other aquatic plants, impassable by human foot, and involved with an atmosphere pregnant with pestilence and death.' (1826) As late as 1935, a traveller through the Levels called it 'a low unhealthy land . . . one of the dreariest, flattest, most monotonous regions in England.' Even now the imprimatur of official taste, designation as an Area of Outstanding Natural Beauty, which is readily distributed among the Scottish islands and across large slices of the Home Counties, has been denied the Levels. Some remains of the idea that beauty needs a third dimension must linger in the offices of the Countryside Commission.

The coming of change and the threat of change has suddenly made the ecology and landscape of a wetland seem more valuable. The disappearance of over 90% of other marshy areas in the country since the war have turned the Somerset Levels into something that matters. This book would not have been written twenty years ago. In that time, two distinct but connected forces have propelled the Levels in a new direction: the developments in drainage technology and the financial structures of modern agriculture. Where change threatens, conservationists trot faithfully after and, in the last decade or so, the Levels have provided the background for one of the bitterest and most complicated arguments between those who want – or need – to impose changes and those who see that as a form of destruction.

The whole economy, farming cycle, plant, insect and bird life of the Somerset Levels has been hinged to the management of water, not its banishment but its tolerated, beneficial presence. Winter floods reseed the meadows, distributing pods around them, dropping what biologists call a 'seed-rain'; they provide habitats for wildfowl which can be shot or lured into decoys; they saturate the peat moors so that the water table stays high through the spring and into the summer. The unique mixture of plants that grow in the meadows are suited to that high water table and could not survive without it. The waders, for which the Levels are an internationally important breeding and stopping-over point, rely on the larvae and small insects which are pushed up near the surface of the fields by the underlying water. One of the few remaining populations of otters in the country survive north of the Poldens and they, of course, depend on the continuing presence of water. Each otter needs eight to ten miles of river bank territory.

It is not a natural landscape but a highly artificial one in which the life-forms now to be found there depend on the annual repetition of many specific human practices. The facile argument, used only by the most rabid of developers, that this is a human system and it would be no destruction for men to alter it, would justify the installation of plate-glass windows in the nave of Chartres Cathedral. It is the human contribution and the continuity of that contribution which is valuable in the Levels, more valuable than anything which might be put in its place. That, anyway, is the contention.

The specific threat is from the modern ability to drain and from the benefits which that improved drainage would bring. The first mechanical steam pumps to be installed in the 1830s marked a crucial change. (Windmills had, for some reason, played virtually no part in earlier schemes.) Drainage no longer depended on gravitation alone and the moors could be rid of their water against the run of the land. The indolence of the drainage authorities, the shortage of money and, to some extent, the technical incompetence of the engineers meant that the full advantages of this development were not realised until the 1960s when, at last, sufficient channels had been dug to carry away the water.

In theory, at least, as a paper by the Agricultural Advisory Council in 1970 suggested, 'These peaty areas

Matt Walker's Newbridge Plant Company laying plastic under-drainage pipes deep into the peat. 'Drainage makes the nation more valuable, doesn't it?'

Lapwings on King's Sedgemoor. Waders like these rely on the high
water table to push their insect food up towards the surface.

Julian Honeybun setting out decoy ducks on a flood for wildfowling. The water in the Levels has always been a curse turned gift, not banished but tolerated and made use of.

The sight of sheep on West Sedgemoor, grazing on a new, reseeded grass ley, would have been impossible even twenty years ago. It depends on the sort of modern drainage technology that makes conservationists squirm.

are potentially as fertile as the Fens, but wet fences and fragmented ownership hold back realisation of the potential.' The arterial drains were already of sufficient capacity to lower the water table over the whole area. Only additional pumping was required. If that were introduced, the Council decided, nearly 100,000 acres of the Levels would be capable of the highest agricultural productivity.

The point is that cereals, root crops and the modern cultivated grasses are unable to grow in wet land or to tolerate submergence in flood water for more than an hour or two. They need under-drains which lower the water table. To instal them is expensive – about £150 an acre – but the return from these crops is worth so much more than the traditional regime of hay followed by grazing that the capital outlay is recovered within nine years, if the field is reseeded with modern grasses, and seven years if put down to cereals. Talk to a drainage man and the arguments can sound convincing enough.

Matt Walker, of the Newbridge Plant Company, has been putting drainage systems into moorland fields for thirty years. 'You've always got to bear in mind that the land doesn't belong to the farmer. It belongs to the nation. The system of security of tenure has allowed the land to be husbanded and preserved over the centuries to *feed* the nation. The encouragement the farmer has is that he can use his own capital and make what profit he can, but he's expected to leave the land better when he dies than when he took it over. Only a few years ago, the land could be taken from you if you didn't farm it properly. You'd be kicked off. That made progressive farmers more progressive, with the reluctant farmers gradually going out.

'The poor farmers were the people who could only afford to buy the poor land and this is where you get people living on the Somerset Levels. Nobody else wanted it. It was flooded every winter. You could hardly make a living on it. You could virtually say that farmers who had to exist until a few years ago on the Levels must have had a very low income indeed. Of course, the minute the technology allowed them to drain better and it was the government's policy to cut down the imports and grow more food in Britain, then obviously it was the policy to encourage the better use of the land and increase the value of the nation's heritage. The food that comes off it is for the benefit of everybody. And when the farmer dies the land moves on to somebody else. It still belongs to the nation. Draining makes the nation more valuable, doesn't it?'

Not only the profit motive, but the air of inheritance, of being the successor to all the enterprise which has made the moors what they are, lies behind Mr Walker's words. If they fail to recognise that the god of increased production has now died, you have to sympathise with his sense of disappointment. What should be a source of pride in the expertise with which he can drop the water table in a field by four or five feet is now widely seen not as an improvement but as a sort of desecration. For a moment though, he can forget the new hostile environment of the conservationists and enthuse over his skills:

'Peat is a soft substance. It's a soup. Ordinary plastic pipes are not successful on peat because the slurry conditions near the pipe are so soft that your pipe gets blocked up and is only partially effective. You've got to get your pipes wrapped. We call it cocos-wrapped. That filters the water and you get a good run in the pipe. Now you've got to get your pipes with a good grade on them, so that the water runs fast through them. You need less pipes if there's a good grade and to get a good grade you've got to put in a deeper ditch, below the Internal Drainage Board levels. Now the cocos keeps the peat out of the inside of the pipes. And the pipe starts running full bore after you've gone three chains into the field, that's sixty yards. You start off dry and then you get a dribble and, as you go on and on, you bring in more and more land and, as your pipe extends, so your pipe becomes surcharged. It can't get out quick enough, so there's a column of water coming out two and a half inches thick from the ends. It'll run like that for twenty-four hours and then it'll gradually drop down because the water table is dropping down in the land.

'You've got to have the water table down roughly two foot so you can actually work it. If you get less, that means the middle of the field is a day late getting dried out, after rain or whatever, than the edge. So if you're in there to farm it, to take silage off or whathaveyou, you'll find you're taking smashing silage cuts off most of the field but in the middle you begin to get bogged because you haven't waited for the extra day.'

The Ministry's dream and the conservationists' nightmare of a lowered water table and a fenland spread of arable fields from one horizon to the other will be delayed, at least, by the structure of land ownership in the Levels. The pattern of tenure is highly fragmented and it is common enough for a farmer to have four different neighbours around one of his fields. Different farmers have different requirements for the management of water in their ditches and no Internal Drainage Board has yet taken the decision to lower the water table over the whole moor. Some farmer or other has always stood out against those improvers who have wanted to benefit from guaranteed corn prices or the high income to be had from vegetables. The idea that all Levels farmers would or even could turn their moorland fields into Lincolnshire prairies exists only in the mind of the more alarmist nature lovers. A conservationist habit of mind, even if it does not go by that name, is not the preserve of outsiders alone. The Levels farmers are cattle men. Over 90% of some parishes are down to permanent grass and the idea that men with this tradition and the equipment that goes with it should suddenly turn to asparagus, barley and daffodils is absurd. They are cow men and cow men they will remain.

Nevertheless, there are pressures for change within the dairy industry itself and those changes, less visible to the outsider, are equally threatening for the ecological value of the Levels. Grass is not simply grass. Grass differs and deep-drained land, with Mr Walker's cocos-wrapped underpipes, will grow the thick blank pelt of cultivated grasses. If you walk across one of these moors in the early summer, before hay or silage has been cut, the difference between improved and unimproved fields is striking.

Where there are no underlying drains, the ground is appreciably softer. It is elastic and bounces back up at each tread, but the difference is sharpest in the quality of the grass.

The new fields are bright, thick and constant, sometimes with an odd, bluish, mineral tinge in the green and so thick that the mat of grass catches at your feet. It is clearly a heavy crop. In the field across the rhyne, where the water table is still high, there is a community of grasses and plants and a variety of duller greens that fringe into the brown. This is the quality of a herb-rich meadow, where plants of different heights make a sweet flowery hay that rattles against your legs at each step, with sudden concentrations of particular flowers, where the floods have dropped seeds and the plants have flourished – a colony of clovers or cowslips, a drifting skein of orchids below the taller hay, the ragged robins and yellow rattles, the clumps of rushes behind which nesting waders can shelter. This is the value of the place. It is not a question of views – what is more beautiful than a field of ripening barley? – but in the close-to difference between the improved and the unimproved, between the precious vegetable sociability of one field and the cloned monotony of the other.

It is exactly that monotony, the reliability of selected strains which can only grow on well-drained soils, which is valuable to the farmer. Draining can also extend the grazing season, lengthening the time that cattle can spend on the moors by six weeks at both the beginning and the end of the year. In a world of rising costs, shrinking margins and quotas on milk production, farmers with an average of just over sixty acres and thirty cows have little choice but to deep-drain and sow the new grasses or fodder beet for winter food. In these circumstances, the publicised image of the greedy farmer is bad and wrong.

Nothing is straightforward. It is not a simple conflict of farming versus wildlife. There is, for example, nothing guaranteed about the strong growth of the new grasses on the drained land. As Dr Johnson of the Nature

Maize being cut for silage near Greylake Foss on King's Sedgemoor. This sort of profitable monoculture can only be maintained with a lowered water table and at the expense of the wet meadowland life that preceded it.

Wheat on West Sedgemoor, to be seen either as the triumph of the modern technology that can drain a place which has been impossibly wet since the sea left it over 6,000 years ago; or the destruction of a rare and now precious resource.

The complicated community of grasses and flowers in an unploughed and unseeded meadow.

Bewick's Swans on West Sedgemoor. To the despair of
conservationists, these birds actually prefer a meadow that has been
drained; it is not so cold.

Conservancy Council says: 'You've got to consider the frost damage. These moors are called moors because they're late land. They're late not because of the water but because they're cold. In the spring, the cold air pours down from the hills and hangs around on the moors. It is simply not true that by draining you are bound to get a good early bite. The opposite is true. Having the water lying on the fields *protects* the grass from any frost die-back. I've seen terrible early frost damage on drained fields. Acres are browned off at the tips. A lot of the farmers are very traditional and would be loath to see that sort of flood benefit go. A winter flood will give a heavy hay crop later in the year, partly through protection and partly through the thickness of the water.'

On the other hand, there is nothing irreversible about digging deep ditches and putting deep drains under a field. If, as has happened on West Sedgemoor, a conservation body buys a patch of improved ground, fails to operate the pump and re-establishes the old regime of a high water table and a late hay cut, those fields will, after a flood or two, return to their old botanical richness, reinfected by seeds from the meadows around them. (This very process was reported to me by one of the more virulently progressive farmers as a scandal typical of the conservationists' negligence on good land.)

On the drainers' side, there is no doubt that some birds, particularly the Bewick's Swans, prefer slightly dryer conditions and Mr Walker claims to have seen one of the very rare waders, a black-tailed godwit, sitting on top of one of his diesel power plants on Earlake Moor, nearly all of which has now gone under the plough.

These are no more than nuances on the edge of a problem in which the main outlines are clear: the economic pressures for dairy farmers to intensify production – and now with quotas to rely less on cattle cake and grow more of their own winter feed – are incompatible with the wetland landscape created by the older techniques. In almost every area the speed, efficiency and ubiquity of modern farming creates conditions hostile to the survival of wetland species.

Without floods, the fields have to be rolled and, as Dr Johnson at the NCC says, 'Moles and nesting waders are not the best of friends with a 2½-ton roller. Farmers have now got to make it a billiard table for their high-speed rotary mowers and forage harvesters.' Ditches and rhynes that used to be hand-cleaned in a five-year cycle, creating a spread of conditions from open water to fairly dense vegetation, where plants and their dependent insects could leapfrog from one section to the next, are now either neglected and filled in, or harshly cleaned out with the insensitive scoop of a Hymac which removes even the embedded rhizomes. The use of nitrogen fertilisers on grass leys makes the water in those ditches that remain too rich, stimulating the growth of a blanket weed that cuts out light and oxygen, killing the other more varied plants that would have rooted and sprouted below. The spraying of ditches can be multiple genocide, while the removal of shrouded willows can obliterate the nest sites of little owls and even ducks resting in their trunks and branches.

Dragonflies and damselflies, water beetles and butterflies, crickets and grasshoppers, breeding waders, the lapwings, curlews, redshank and snipe, the famous godwits and the whimbrels that use the moors as a staging post during their migration, the mute swans you find on rushy nests in the mouths of ditches – all that will go if the wetness goes. These animals and plants depend on a mixture of land and water, on a softness for example in the springtime earth, after the floods have gone, through which the chicks can poke for their worms and leatherjackets. If the wetness goes – not simply open water, but a landscape that is sodden – something that is beautiful in a discreet, connected and inconceivably complicated way will have been lost.

There is a horizon below which the genetic pool becomes too small, where the interchange between different populations is so disrupted that decline becomes inevitable. Dr Johnson at the NCC thinks that for the populations of breeding waders and otters in the Levels that critical point may now have been reached.

Jimmy Hartland, cattleman on West Sedgemoor, is famous for the well-being of his cows.

You will find many people in Somerset who pooh-pooh this doomwatching. One joke current among the farmers at the moment claims that the NCC feels so sorry for the poor little birds on West Sedgemoor that they are planning to bring in a multi-million pound hot-water pipeline from the nuclear power station at Hinkley Point so that the little things can keep warm in the winter time. Mr Walker the drainer has little patience with conservationists who claim that all but 10% of the Levels has been spoilt in some way. 'These moors have hardly been touched yet. And why is it every time you hear some boy scout spouting on about wetlands, it's always the last place in Europe, the last place in the world, when you know damn fine it's not? You know damn fine that across the hill there's another moor with the same species growing or twittering or buzzing its little heart out. It makes you spit. All these retired folk from Kenya or Rhodesia with some idea of what the old country should be like with no idea that people have to make a living out of that old country. And what's it done to the farmers and the drainage men? I'll tell you: we're the endangered species now. You should see us. We've all got copies of the Wildlife and Countryside Act 1981 at the bedside now, seeing if there is any mention in there of the Greater Crested Farmer or the Lesser Spotted Drainage Engineer. You look in any of these farmhouses round here at eleven at night and they'll all be reading a couple of chapters of the barmy thing before dropping off to sleep. It's not barmy. It's worse than that. It's criminal. But I'll tell you what. You wait for a change in the weather like they've had in Ethiopia. You wait till it starts raining a little bit more in Somerset and then we'll see what happens with the wheat shortages and where the calls for more drainage start coming from then.'

The confrontation came to a head over West Sedgemoor. It is one of the lowest and wettest moors. Just outside living memory boys kept gaggles of geese out in the middle. It was good for little else. There were pools of open water standing on the moor until the early years of this century. A pump was installed during the war and withies, corn and flax were grown on the belt of clay surrounding the peaty middle. Even so, the farmers in the West Sedgemoor IDB voted not to work the pumps in the winter time. They liked it wet.

The Ministry classified the moor as Grade 2 land which means that, given deep drainage, it could become a 2,500-acre prairie of winter wheat. In the early 1970s, the Wessex Water Authority proposed a scheme for the moor in which a wide new river like the King's Sedgemoor Drain would be cut straight down the middle. Every field could be deep drained, the water table could be pushed out of sight and the money from corn intervention prices would start rolling in. 'Weren't we all delighted!'

The scheme did not work out as planned. The fields in the middle of the moor would benefit most but, because of an antiquated rating system, their owners would pay least towards it. A revision of the rating system would have cost a fortune in legal fees. On the other hand, the owners of those middle fields did not like the prospect of all the rubbish from the new main drain being dumped on their land. And other farmers simply did not want to change because peat swells and shrinks according to its wetness and they were unsure if any scheme would survive for long in this mobile environment. In the end nothing happened.

The ghost of improvement had been raised and there was no guarantee that the farmers would not change their minds in the future. The Royal Society for the Protection of Birds began to buy land on the moor and then lease it back on the condition that it should continue to be farmed in the traditional way – winter flooding, high water table in summer, no fertilisers, no reseeding, a late hay cut in July. The farmers were delighted. The RSPB, loaded with money from subscriptions, could pay far more for the land than anyone else and with the new capital the farmers could buy much better land off the moor. Their farm businesses expanded, their surroundings were as beautiful as ever, a new sense of value was attached to the Levels and everyone was happy. Nothing had been imposed – you either sold to the RSPB or you didn't – and none of the old independence of the moors-men, which had stood out against interference

Near Moorland on the Parrett.

In Meare.

Max King's corrugated house in Sharpham.

In Isle Brewers.

since the thirteenth century, which had cut the monastic banks, thrown down their weirs, thwarted royal schemes for drainage and denial of their common rights, which had left the churches empty and packed the chapels, which had created an inter-reliant and self-sufficient community – none of that had yet been challenged.

The Wildlife and Countryside Act was passed in 1981. It gave the Nature Conservancy Council new powers to create Sites of Special Scientific Interest (SSSIs) where restrictions would be placed on farming practices and where the NCC could negotiate management agreements with the farmer to compensate him for any loss of income the restrictions might involve. (It is a measure of the change the last few years have brought to the Levels that an entirely new vocabulary and a weird set of acronyms are now needed to describe a place that was previously understandable in terms of water, cows, grass, people, willows, cider and eels.) The RSPB, the Somerset Trust for Nature Conservation (STNC) and the Mid-Somerset Naturalists (M-SN) put great pressure on the NCC to 'notify' – that is designate as an SSSI – all 2,500 acres of West Sedgemoor. Individual farmers on the moor had already made use of Mr Walker's drains and pumps and now there were potatoes growing on the moor. Something had to be done.

Dr Johnson explains. 'First you must understand this: there is no point in the agricultural development of marginal land to produce vast surpluses that cost very much more to dispose of than the price, acre for acre, of a management agreement by which the surpluses never arise and by which the inherent qualities of the place are preserved and even enhanced. That is the background.

'Now. When the row over West Sedgemoor blew up, the NCC was lumbered with an Act that was appallingly drafted. It was very new and very complex. The NCC was under pressure from all sides. It was underfunded. There were only two permanent staff here at the time. They had a workload which nearly cracked both of them up. There was this major arterial scheme hanging over the moor. STNC and RSPB were on our backs. The great god Treasury had not published any financial guidelines for the way the compensation was going to be drawn up, how it was going to be calculated. We had *no* idea. We were also aware of the three-month loophole between notification and the legal sanctions coming into force. We knew there was an enormous amount of animosity towards the conservation bodies because conservation at that time was not accepted by the farming communities *at all*. So: there is the possibility of a lucrative scheme hanging in the background for some people. Do we risk putting off notification until we've seen everyone – with the shortage of staff that would have taken years – and risk enormous site damage, as had happened else-where? (Without, remember, being able to explain to the farmers exactly how much they were going to get in compensation.) Or do we go ahead and notify straight-away with no informal consultation at all? It was a question of saving the moor or saving our relationship with the farmers.'

The smell of panic, even at this distance, is strong enough. The NCC went ahead in 1982 and notified all the farmers on West Sedgemoor that their land was now to be part of a Site of Special Scientific Interest. In all the villages around West Sedgemoor, in the farms on the edge of the moor itself, the letters of notification arrived. They were necessarily couched in the imperious language of the Act, which is neither diplomatic nor tactful. They gave the farmers a long list of operations which might damage the botanical and ornithological interest of the SSSI. 'You are required by the Wildlife and Countryside Act 1981,' each farmer was told, 'to give NCC written notice of an intention to carry out any of the listed operations.' It was like telling a man how to treat his wife and it detonated an explosion of indignation and rage of which the echoes can still be heard today.

'I think they're a little bit touched,' Dick House says. 'We had lived a peaceful, quiet, ordinary life. There was no one to interfere with us. Then in comes this letter of notification from Mr Rob Williams of the Nature Conservancy Council telling us what we could and couldn't do. No sprays, no rolling, no chain-harrowing, no average, everyday work of the land. My grandfather always said to me that if you want to be a good farmer you want to be a good nursemaid: keep a clean face and *a dry bottom*. And then old Rob Williams comes in and says NO.'

Chris and Anne Coate, the withy-growers at Meare Green, found all their withy beds included in the SSSI. *Anne:* It was the clumsy way it was done. They shouldn't have done it like that. Poor old Rob Williams came in here and he didn't even know what a willow was or anything to do with it. Obviously he upset us. He didn't stop and look, did he? He was adamant no one could spray any more. I shall never forget that poor man coming in, all up in arms. It's turned out we can keep spraying, thank goodness. There wouldn't be a withy business if you didn't spray. But you go down into our withy beds when they're high and you'll find pheasants in there. I've seen roe deer in a withy bed and there have been masses of little voles. We don't spray the ditches or the rhynes, but you wouldn't get a kestrel in the withy bed if the spray killed everything, would you?

Chris: I wouldn't say we felt happy about the SSSI. A Labour government would be heavier on the conservationist line and, to tell you the truth, we're frightened that SSSIs will be the first land to be nationalised.

Anne: We're trying to keep the oldest craft in Somerset going. We employ ten, a dozen people in the village – more if you count the people packing the charcoal. It's just as important as the wildlife. I don't see how the wildlife need be at risk anyway if we continue. And surely this is the conservation of a craft? But they won't accept this. They've got blinkers on. All they think of is birds and flowers, birds and flowers.

Chris: And otters.

Anne: And otters. But there hasn't been an otter down there for donkey's years.

The farmers began to organise their opposition. Two local Tory MPs with influence, Tom King and Edward du Cann, were brought into play. A large open air meeting was held outside the Black Smock on the edge of Sedgemoor itself. Three stuffed dummies of Rob Williams, Sir Ralph Verney, the director of the NCC, and of

John Humphreys, the local RSPB man, were hanged and then burnt in front of the television cameras. One farmer got hold of an old American tank and parked it outside the pub. A great show was made of burning the notification letters themselves. It was kept from the press that these were photocopies and that the originals, in line with true Levels common sense, were filed away. There was a great deal of standing around in the mildly festive air.

The NFU, terrified that the exuberant resistance from the Sedgemoor farmers would bring even tougher legislation, tried to tone things down. An editorial in *The Somerset Farmer* talked about 'forebearance, understanding, and . . . a flexible, diplomatic approach'. It went on: 'And equally, it would be highly regrettable were farmers to attempt to pre-empt designation by rushing in with the drainers.' Tom King came down and made a speech in Burrow Bridge. 'There are forces in our Society,' he said, like a rural McCarthy, 'who would like to see compulsion, confiscation of your rights and the imposition of rigid controls. If we in Somerset fail to make this Act work, we run the risk of letting in something very much worse.' There was little applause and West Sedgemoor was indeed eventually designated as an SSSI. But King made sure the Levels men had some blood. Sir Ralph Verney, after finally approving the designation of the moor, was sacked.

The bitterness of the dispute has lasted and the name of Rob Williams is not one to conjure with in farmhouses on the Levels. The men on the West Sedgemoor Drainage Board have refused to allow the Somerset representative of the RSPB to join them, alarmed that he might try to force up the summer penning levels. Instead, the Board taunts the NCC by suggesting a drop in that level of a single inch – actually insignificant, but enough to produce another flutter of panic among the conservationists. In fact, farmers are quite impotent against the Act which provides their bedtime reading. It equips the NCC with quite a bludgeon. If the farmer will not make a management agreement, and if the Ministry then imposes a Nature Conservation Order, and the

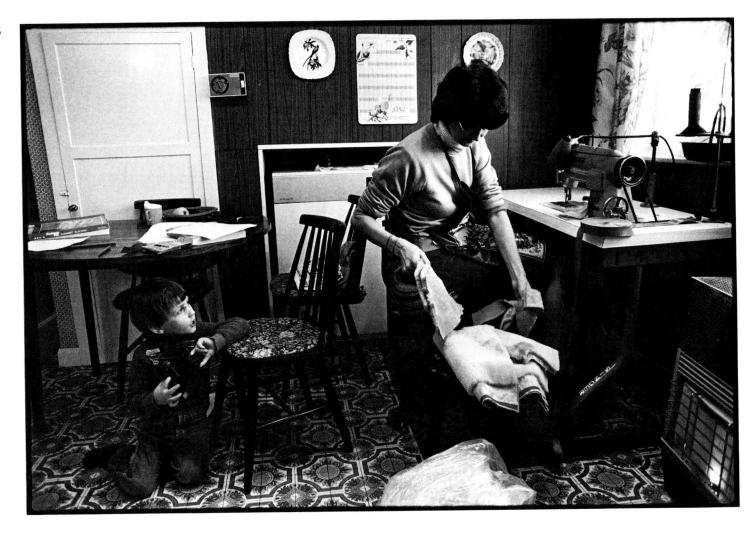

Sandra Lovelace making sheepskin jackets at home in Walton.

Tony Mailey designs printed circuit boards in Cocklake.

farmer still goes ahead with draining, he can be fined £1000, with a possible further fine of £100 a day as long as the pumps are kept working. It is against that background and the problems Secretary of State for the Environment has in overturning any NCC decision, that the designation of the Moor went through. The man could be expunged; the decision could not.

Loathing of the conservationists if not of conservationism spread to other parts of the Levels. As Stan Durston of Meare says: 'If they weren't quite so damned greedy! Why can't they do with the worked out peat land? They could have it porridgy. It could be soft and wet – there's your wetland for you and we could get on with the farming.

'Now Hitler was a dictator, and we don't want too many of them, do we? I spent six years of my life fighting Hitler and the whole purpose of my fighting, and a lot of my friends dying, was freedom. And I'm damned if I'm going to be dictated to. This land wasn't got by any . . . I had to lose a lot of sweat to get it. So nobody's coming in and start dictating to me. That Williams (*he laughs*), he rubbed people up the wrong way, didn't he? Coming in here waving your finger at people.

'I don't want to see a rape of the countryside, but I'll tell you something: I was out there the other day, I was shooting over my land as it happens, and this fine fellow was walking all over it, flushing everything out. So I said to him, "What the hell do you think you're doing?" And do you know what he said? "I'm a conservationist." I ask you. They walk across there as if they've got the deeds on the place, some of them. Most of these do-gooders are all very generous with other people's property and money. I'd like to see what would happen if we decided that the bottom ten yards of their garden was a site of Special Scientific Excitement, or what have you. That would be something. "I'm very sorry, Mr Williams, you can't go in there now. You'll be disturbing the worms. And that sparrow over there, well it turns out to be a very special sort of Outer Mongolian Marsh Sparrow which you didn't happen to know about." Then we'd see the sparks fly.

'The archaeologists have got the right approach. There's no laying down the law with them. They say: "Can we dig this piece of trackway here, this little bit there?" And the peat men have always been most cooperative. That's the word. That's the way to keep the Somerset Levels. But I've got a word for them too: "Don't push your luck. Don't bite the hand that feeds you." Because now even the archaeologists are getting in on this insistence business. They tell us we're pumping too much, that the water table's dropping in the peat and the trackways are rotting in the ground where it's drier. But look at it this way. Nobody can dig the peat until it's dry. And until you dig the peat, you can't find the trackways. All right. So we do what they suggest. We stop pumping. We stop digging peat. And we stop finding trackways. Then everyone is sitting very pretty, aren't they? But I'll tell you what. Peat extractors might stop telling the archaeologists about the trackways they find. Then the great story of archaeology in the Somerset Levels would come to a pretty smart end. I don't believe it's really that serious. It's not as bad as they make out. They're just seeing how far they can push us. But I tell you: you can get bow-legged carrying these people about on your back.

'If you're really talking about the future of the Levels, it depends on the dairy farmers. There's two sorts of farmer: farmers with cows with long necks and farmers with cows with short necks. The younger, modern, pushy farmers, their cows have got long necks. They can reach the water, no matter how far down it is. They're the ones who make cow-drinks in the edge of the rhynes. That's not a new thing. It's as old as the hills. It's just that most of them have been too bloody tired to do it. They've been penning it up level with the bank. And of course their grass roots stop at the water table an inch or two down and you get a

The slaughterhouse in Ashcott. Cows that had 'gone screw' from the fluke in the Levels water used to be sent to the lions in Bristol zoo.

rubbishy little bit of grass on top. But you drop that water a foot or two, the roots head down towards it through the new ground and the grass does a damn sight better. You've got to have a bit of push.

'Anyway the best water for cows isn't ditch water. It's tap-water, out the mains. All moor-water has got fluke in it. It gets in the liver and starts eating the liver out. You can get fluke by eating watercress out of a rhyne. Once a cow's got it, she won't die but she'll never do. You'd see cattle go "screw" with fluke. They were thin and poor and you'd see the ribs showing through. They used to send them to the knackermen. People used to *live* out of drowned animals and fluke. They'd always have one cow a year that went screw. And she always went for the lions up at Bristol Zoo. Now that's your old "Life on the Levels" for you. That's the life of farmers who've got cows with short necks. And we've got to leave that behind. I've got piped water into troughs in most of my fields and good drains under them. We're not old rustics out in the sticks here, you know. You've got to have a bit of a push in a place. And we've got to leave all that rubbishy, non-productive scrubland behind. You could never do anything with it. It was waterlogged and boggy.'

'Waterlogged and boggy' means one thing when you are sitting at an NCC desk and the opposite if you are driving a forage harvester. The confrontation is utterly symmetrical, using the same words to opposite effect. But crucial changes have occurred since the great West Sedgemoor affair. Most important has been the shift in the Ministry's attitude to farming in general. The decades of insistence on production at any cost have given way to a more balanced approach. Quotas have been imposed on milk production. The grants available to farmers for land drainage have now dropped from 37.5% of the cost to 15%. Some cuts in corn prices have already occurred; others are forecast.

One measure of the effect of these changes is the lukewarm reception given by Levels farmers to the grand schemes proposed by Wessex Water Authority for improved drainage in the Brue and Parrett basins. In a climate of agricultural retraction, the increased water rates these schemes would impose would cancel out any predicted benefit. The reputation of the more flamboyant improvers, who have turned large slices of Earlake Moor over to maize, have now sunk. 'Shake em, see what they got,' one of their more traditional neighbours said. 'You can borrow anything you like, can't you,' he added and then described the God-given order of things. 'There's a farm down at the bottom that can look to dairy cows. The next one up can grow corn. And the one up above that again on the hill will have sheep. And you don't want to go messing about with that.' A new conservatism has taken hold in the Levels, joining hands with its ancient predecessor.

On their side, the NCC have trod more carefully. No other SSSIs were notified for nearly three years after West Sedgemoor. Extra staff were taken on, firm financial guidelines were established and very long talks were held with each landowner before the famous letters were sent out. Dr Johnson maintains that Levels farmers now 'recognise that wetland wildlife has all but disappeared. . . . The spirit of cooperation on the moors is alive and well. Almost every farmer now realises that conservation has got to be done.' This change in heart has, perhaps not by coincidence, accompanied the change in economic climate for farmers. In the new chill, the promise of a management agreement, guaranteed for twenty years, looks like the safest of havens. The conservationists, from being the great subversive threat to the welfare of the farmer, can now be seen, with government money in hand, as the best of friends. 'Conservation blight' – a drop in the capital value of land inside the SSSIs – has not materialised and farmers are now hungry for management agreements. By the end of 1985, the NCC had notified the owners in another six SSSIs in the Levels, nearly 7,000 acres spread across the moors. Consultation was well advanced on another 2,700 acres north of the Poldens. When the programme is complete, there might be nearly 16,000 acres of the Levels under the supervision of the NCC, with 1,500 or 2,000 acres of that directly owned by the state in the shape of four or five National Nature Reserves.

It is the strangest of conclusions. Men who are heirs to the most independent of traditions come to guarantee the landscape of that tradition and its social structures, based on the small family farm, by renouncing their rights to change and by accepting payment for that renunciation from a government body. Many of the management agreements actually involve turning the clock back – abandoning herbicides, pesticides and chemical fertiliser; returning to the hand clearance of ditches, leaving deep drains that are already in place unused – all in exchange for government money.

The Levels will become at the same time the most traditional and the most modern of places in which the landscape, the way of life and even the old attitudes quite genuinely continue to exist but all guaranteed with the uniquely modern paraphernalia of NCC, STNC, RSPB, NNRs, SSSIs, management agreements, interim payments, three-year reviews, the Countryside Forum, the Community Council for Somerset, the County Council Structure Plan, the Water Space Amenity Commission, the Somerset County Council Countryside Subject Plan – Landscape (Levels and Moors) Consultative Report of Survey, Draft Plan and Framework for Implementation.

In the NCC offices outside Taunton, there is a new sort of map of the Levels. It is the filing system. Row on row of folders, hung from metal racks, detail the holdings and practices, the responses and attitudes of each of the farmers in the special areas, field by field, objection by objection, agreement by agreement. In its care and detail,

it is a sort of parody of the real landscape outside of meadows and rhynes, of clyses, sluices and drains, of the mixture of cooperation and imposition which has always been the hallmark of life on the Levels.

It must not be overstated. Most farms remain free of restriction and ecologically degraded in some way or other. In many ways, the Levels continue to play their traditional role, outside the mainstream of life. House prices – that most sensitive index of implied worth – are lower on the moors than in the villages on the high ground encircling them. Montacute is a universe away from Burrow Bridge. The population of the Levels is less mobile than in other places and there are fewer retired newcomers than in most villages. Young families can afford to buy the cheaper houses and the age profile is healthier than in most of Somerset. Villages do not on the whole consist of ex-colonels manoeuvring for position on the parish council – although little else is said to happen in North Curry nowadays.

There will always be the place itself, as level as its name, and reliably odd. That unapproachable strangeness – vulgarised, made use of and eventually bypassed in the Arthur–Guinevere–Holy Thorn–Mouth of Hell Mystery Business at Glastonbury, where a fast food store called Avalot has now opened – will always be the same. And as you slide down the line of the Great Western Railway that cuts off the bottom of West Sedgemoor, or take twenty minutes or so to cross this flat wet land on the M5, en route to the Cornish fishing village or the Devon beach, look out of the window for a minute, beyond the present willows, and remember the poise of the heron and the slip of the eel.

On Glastonbury Tor. *The fast food store called Avalot is down below.*

The M5 at Dunwear. A sort of indifference to the modern world.

SOURCES

The two outstandingly good books about the Somerset Levels are:

Michael Williams, *The Drainage of the Somerset Levels*, 1970

Bernard Storer, *The Natural History of the Somerset Levels*, 2nd edition, 1985

Among the other sources I have consulted are:

Anonymous, *A True Report of Certain Wonderful Overflowings of Waters, now lately in Summmersetshire etc.*, 1607

A. Bulleid, *The Lake Village of Somerset*, 4th edition, 1949

J. M. Coles and B. J. Orme, *Prehistory of the Somerset Levels*, Somerset Levels Project, 1980

J. W. E. Conybeare, *Alfred in the Chroniclers*, 1900

Stan Davies and Rob Jarman, *Wildlife of the Somerset Levels and Moors*, no date

C. V. Dawe and J. E. Blundell, *An Economic Survey of the Somerset Willow Growing Industry*, 1932

R. W. Dunning, *Christianity in Somerset*, 1976

David M. Forrest, *Eel Capture, Culture, Processing and Marketing*, 1976

Michael Havinden, *The Somerset Landscape*, 1981

Desmond Hawkins, *Avalon and Sedgemoor*, 1982

F. G. Heath, *Peasant Life in the West of England*, 1880

W. Johnson, *Survey of the Central Somerset Lowlands*, 1965

Nature Conservancy Council, *The Somerset Wetlands Project*, 1977

Richard North, *Wild Britain*, 1983

G. R. Quaife, *Wanton Wenches and Wayward Wives*, 1979

Somerset County Council, *Countryside Subject Plan – Landscape (Levels and Moors) Consultative Report of Survey*, 1981

Somerset Levels and Moors Plan (Draft), 1983

Somerset Levels and Moors Strategy, Framework for Implementation, 1984

Peat in Central Somerset, 1967

Somerset Levels Project, *Papers*, annual

T. Stuart-Menteath, *Somerset*, 1938

B. M. Swainson, *Rural Settlement in Somerset*, 1935

F.-W. Tesch, *The Eel*, 2nd edition, 1977

Keith Thomas, *Religion and the Decline of Magic*, 1971

W. M. Wigfield, *The Monmouth Rebellion*, 1980

as well as issues of the *Bridgwater Mercury* and the *Burnham on Sea and Highbridge Gazette and Express* of various dates.

Harold Hembrow and Charlie Langford after a hail storm on West Sedgemoor.

INDEX

(**bold type** indicates illustration)

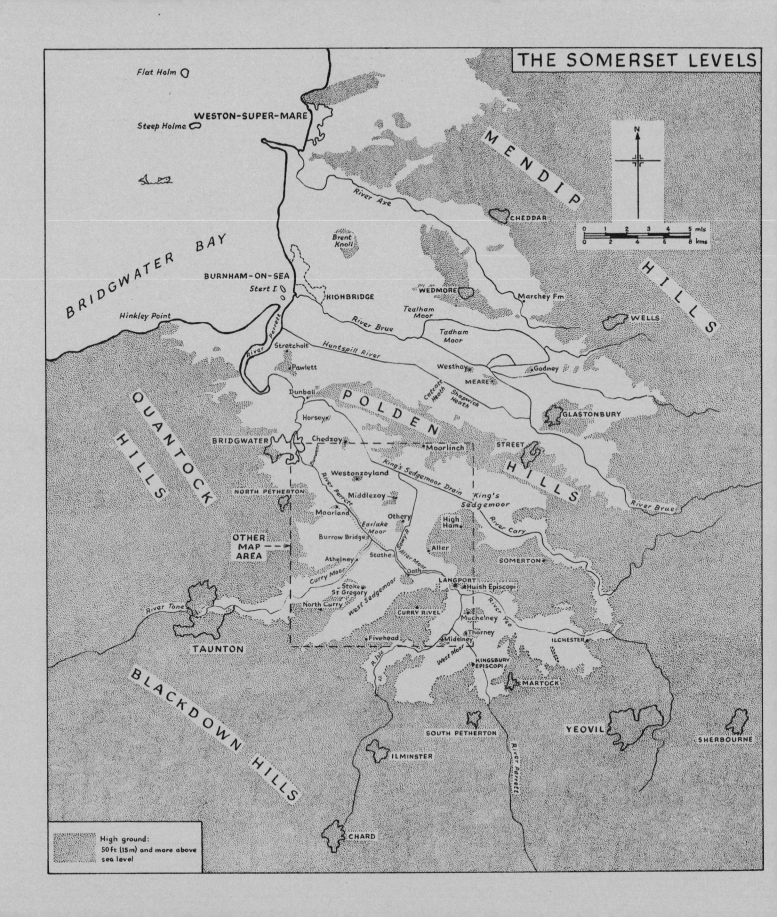

THE SOMERSET LEVELS

Flat Holm

WESTON-SUPER-MARE

Steep Holme

MENDIP

River Axe

CHEDDAR

HILLS

N

0 1 2 3 4 5 mls
0 2 4 6 8 kms

BRIDGWATER BAY

Brent
Knoll

BURNHAM-ON-SEA

Stert I.

HIGHBRIDGE

WEDMORE

Marchey Fm

WELLS

Hinkley Point

River Brue

Tealham
Moor

Stretcholt

Huntspill River

Tadham
Moor

River Parrett

Pawlett

Westhay

Godney

Dunball

Catcott Heath

Shapwick
Heath

MEARE

POLDEN

GLASTONBURY

Horsey

QUANTOCK

BRIDGWATER

Chedzoy

Moorlinch

STREET

HILLS

Westonzoyland

King's Sedgemoor Drain

HILLS

NORTH PETHERTON

Middlezoy

'King's
Sedgemoor

River Parrett

Moorland

Othery

High
Ham

River Cary

OTHER
MAP
AREA

Earlake
Moor

Burrow Bridge

Aller

SOMERTON

Sowy R

Athelney

Stathe

Salter Moor

Curry Moor

Oath

LANGPORT

Huish Episcopi

Stoke
St Gregory

West Sedgemoor

Muchelney

River Yeo

North Curry

CURRY RIVEL

Thorney

ILCHESTER

River Tone

Fivehead

Mideleny

R. Isle

West Moor

KINGSBURY
EPISCOPI

TAUNTON

MARTOCK

BLACKDOWN

SOUTH PETHERTON

YEOVIL

SHERBOURNE

River Parrett

HILLS

ILMINSTER

CHARD

High ground:
50 ft (15m) and more above
sea level